The Martyred Christian

DATE DUE

THE MARTYRED

160 READINGS FROM

CHRISTIAN

Dietrich Bonhoeffer

Selected and Edited by Joan Winmill Brown

COLLIER BOOKS
MACMILLAN PUBLISHING COMPANY
New York

COLLIER MACMILLAN PUBLISHERS
London

Macmillan Publishing Company
866 Third Avenue, New York, N.Y. 10022
Collier Macmillan Canada, Inc.

Library of Congress Cataloging in Publication Data
Bonhoeffer, Dietrich, 1906-1945.
The martyred Christian.
Originally published: New York: Macmillan; London:
Collier Macmillan, c1983.
Bibliography: p. 220
1. Theology—Addresses, essays, lectures.   I. Brown,
Joan Winmill.   II. Title.
BR85.B725   1985   230'.044   85-5932
ISBN 0-02-084020-9

Macmillan books are available at special discounts for bulk purchases for sales
promotions, premiums, fund-raising, or educational use. For details, contact:
Special Sales Director
Macmillan Publishing Company
866 Third Avenue
New York, N.Y. 10022

First Collier Books Edition 1985
10 9 8 7 6 5 4 3 2

Printed in the United States of America

The author gratefully acknowledges permission to reprint
Abridged excerpts from pages 64, 65, 104-106, 110 in *Christ the Center* by Dietrich
Bonhoeffer. Translated by Edwin Robertson. Copyright © 1947 by Christian
Kaiser Verlag in Bonhoeffer's *Gesammelte Schriften*, Vols. 1-4. Copyright ©
1966, 1978 in the English translation as Christology by William Collins, Sons,
& Co., Ltd., and Harper & Row, Publishers, Inc. Reprinted by permission
of Harper & Row, Publishers, Inc., and William Collins, Sons, & Co., Ltd.
Abridged excerpts from pages 17, 20, 27–28, 40–41, 99 in *Life Together* by Dietrich
Bonhoeffer. Translated by John W. Doberstein. Copyright, 1954, by Harper
& Row, Publishers, Inc. Reprinted by permission of Harper and Row, Pub-
lishers, Inc.
Excerpts from *The Cost of Discipleship* by Dietrich Bonhoeffer, translation © SCM
Press 1948, 1959; *Ethics* by Dietrich Bonhoeffer, translation © SCM Press 1955;
Letters and Papers from Prison by Dietrich Bonhoeffer, The Enlarged Edition,
translation © SCM Press 1953, 1967, 1971; *Creation and Fall* by Dietrich
Bonhoeffer, translation © SCM Press 1959; *Creation and Temptation* by Dietrich
Bonhoeffer, translation © SCM Press 1959, 1966 (containing *Creation and Fall*
and *Temptation* in one volume). Reprinted by permission of SCM Press Ltd.
and Macmillan Publishing Company.
Excerpt from *No Rusty Swords* by Dietrich Bonhoeffer, translated by Edwin
Robertson and John Bowden, translation © William Collins Sons & Company
Ltd., 1965. Published by William Collins Sons & Co., Ltd., and Christian
Kaiser Verlag.

This book is dedicated
to the Bonhoeffer family and all Christians
who suffered and were martyred,
during the years of the Third Reich.

Contents

Foreword

AT DAWN, on April 9, 1945, Dietrich Bonhoeffer was led by his guards down the steps leading to the execution area at the Flossenburg concentration camp in Germany. Only a few days before the Allies were to liberate the camp, the Nazis, at the express order of Heinrich Himmler, hanged this so-called "enemy of the state."

The leaders of the Third Reich were mistaken, however, in thinking that they could ever silence Bonhoeffer. His writings live on to enrich us spiritually, and to tell us what was required of those who lived as Christians amid the horrors of Nazi Germany. For many people the Germans of the 1930s and 1940s represent the "complete enemy," and little thought is given to those Christians who suffered for their religious beliefs. But the prisons of Europe were filled with Christians who refused to obey Adolf Hitler. These men and women were martyred because of their stand for Jesus Christ and His Church. One such Christian was Dietrich Bonhoeffer.

Bonhoeffer was born in 1906 and was recognized as an accomplished scholar while still in his twenties. He received his licentiate in theology in Berlin in 1927 and served a brief pastorate in Barcelona. He returned to Germany and the academic world to finish his habilitation thesis, entitled *Act and Being,* before traveling to America as an exchange student in 1930. Bonhoeffer returned to his native country the following year and became a lecturer in theology at the Berlin University; the lectures he delivered on the first three chapters of the book of Genesis were to become the exceedingly popular *Creation and Fall.*

Bonhoeffer's sojourn in America had opened his eyes politically, and he began to see with concern that Nazi influence was seeping into the politics of Germany. Hitler despised Christians, saying, reportedly, "You can do anything you want with them. They will submit...they are insignificant little people, submissive as dogs...." When he became the Führer in 1933, Hitler began a campaign of persecution and demoralization of the German Christian Church. Resisting the members of the Reich Church who were loyal to Hitler was a small group that came to be called the "Confessing Church," and Dietrich Bonhoeffer was one of its most vocal ministers. This Confessing Church split off from the Reich Church, and became one of the few institutions to oppose Hitler.

Bonhoeffer's disgust for Hitler and the submissive Reich Church moved him to accept a pastorate in London, where he developed a close friendship with George Bell, the bishop of Chichester. Bonhoeffer felt that the opinion of the worldwide church could have tremendous influence on events in Germany, and he kept Bell informed about the political climate created by the Nazis. Six years before he would be executed, Bonhoeffer wrote, "When Christ calls a man, he bids him come and die." Bishop Bell said of him, "There are different kinds of dying, it is true; but the essence of discipleship is contained in these words." He went on to say, "Dietrich was a martyr many times before he died. He was one of the first as well as one of the bravest witnesses against idolatry. He understood what he chose, when he chose resistance...He was crystal clear in his convictions; and young as he was, and humble-minded as he was, he saw the truth, and spoke it with complete absence of fear..."

When Bonhoeffer returned to Germany in 1935, he founded an illegal seminary of the Confessing Church at Finkenwalde, and during this period he wrote *The Cost of Discipleship*. The book is a brilliant exposition on the Sermon on the Mount. Bonhoeffer believed that these words of Jesus Christ were a source of power that could destroy the Nazi Reich, provided that the Church lived uncompromisingly by them, preaching fearlessly against what was fast becoming a godless dictatorship. In *The Cost of Discipleship*, students heard for the first time the terms *cheap grace* and *costly grace*. "Cheap grace is the deadly enemy of the church," said Bonhoeffer. "We are fighting today for costly grace."

During the Finkenwalde period Bonhoeffer produced two other exceptional books. One, *Life Together*, reveals the secret to living together as Christians, and is character-istic of the apostle Paul in its direct and practical approach. The second is entitled *Temptation* and deals with the daily human struggle against temptation and with the assur-ance that it can be overcome through Jesus Christ.

As Bonhoeffer continued to work for the Confessing Church, he spoke out repeatedly against the discrimina-tion and persecution of the Jews. Although the Nazis threatened anyone who dared to "interfere in politics," Bonhoeffer would not be silenced, and he implored the Church to exercise its commission, taking as his text Proverbs 31:8: "Open your mouth for the dumb!" But after the horror of the "Crystal Night," when synagogues were burned and the Jewish community terrorized, the Confessing Church lost the courage to make any more public statements.

At this time Bonhoeffer's brother-in-law, Hans von Dohnanyi, who was the personal assistant to the minister of justice, became active in a military plot to overthrow Hitler. Dohnanyi confided in Bonhoeffer, who thus became an accessory to the plan, a crime that carried the death penalty. When Hitler's armies marched into Bohemia and Moravia in 1939, Bonhoeffer was no longer able to speak in public, and he accepted an invitation to take a sabbatical in America. He hoped that there he could carry on the work of his Church and complete his study of ethics. Before long, however, he realized how much he missed his homeland and those who were actively resisting the Reich. Although it meant certain persecution, he decided to return to Germany. He felt he would have no right to participate in the reconstruction of his country if he did not share also in her tribulation.

Shortly after Bonhoeffer's return, his brother-in-law arranged for him to be sent to Munich, where he joined the staff of the Abwehr (the intelligence bureau) as a civilian employee. Now in the inner circle of the resistance movement, Bonhoeffer stayed in a Benedictine monastery at Ettal and worked on his study of ethics while awaiting Abwehr assignments, which allowed him to travel outside Germany; he seized every opportunity to work for the Confessing Church. Regarded highly in ecumenical circles, Bonhoeffer traveled to Switzerland, Sweden, Norway, and Italy. He also relayed news about the resistance to London and carried information back to Germany. On one of his trips to Switzerland he was able to take a small group of Jews to safety. While in Sweden, Bonhoeffer contacted his old friend Bishop Bell, to whom he gave information about the intended coup. The bishop communicated the details to Britain's foreign minister, Anthony Eden; Eden felt that the communication might disguise a peace feeler from the Nazis, and so refused to send any reply.

Plans were then made for the assassination of Hitler. Bonhoeffer was horrified at the thought of murder, but he knew he could not stand by to witness the annihilation of so many people. As a minister he said he felt he must do more than comfort the relatives of those killed by the drunken driver; he must seize the wheel.

In 1943 the net around Bonhoeffer began to tighten. An Abwehr conspirator was arrested, and under torture, revealed the names of the members of the resistance. Bonhoeffer was warned that his telephone was being tapped, and when on April 5 his father came to tell him that two men were waiting to speak to him, Bonhoeffer knew what would happen. Calmly he went to meet the representatives of the Gestapo and left with them, never to return to his family home.

On his desk were the copious notes for his work on ethics. His close friend, Eberhard Bethge, painstakingly pieced together these notes, and saw to their publication in 1945 under the title *Ethics*. In *Ethics*, Bonhoeffer presents the case for the spirit of Jesus Christ permeating the everyday lives of those who believe in Him. All decisions, actions, relationships with family and neighbors, must be inspired by His presence; responsibility cannot be excused away. As Christians we must stand for all our Saviour lived and died for, in the triumph of the Resurrection.

After his arrest Bonhoeffer was taken to Tegel Prison, where he was tortured and interrogated. Not once did he implicate any of his family or other members of the Abwehr. Of the sessions he would only say that they were "disgusting." At first he spent weeks in solitary confinement; although the guards were forbidden to talk to political prisoners, many of them befriended Bonhoeffer, smuggling letters in and out of prison. One guard even arranged a visit from Bonhoeffer's sister. Because of the guards and Eberhard Bethge, we are able to share Bonhoeffer's experiences in *Letters and Papers from Prison*. In his letters Bonhoeffer shows us that, although separated from those he loved—friends, family, and fiancée— he was still capable of joy. The narrow confines of his prison cell provided a frame for a rich intellectual Christian life. Nor did he lose his sense of humor: Bonhoeffer referred to his experience in prison as "an unexpected sabbatical term."

In Tegel Prison he was able to minister to his neighbors and to demonstrate that Jesus Christ was all that He had promised, even amid vileness and suffering. Others looked to him for help and comfort, seeing in him a tower of strength.

In October 1943 Bonhoeffer was transferred to the Gestapo bunker in Prinz-Albrecht-Strasse and underwent further interrogation, never betraying his fellow conspirators. While Bonhoeffer was in solitary confinement, the building above the bunker was destroyed in an Allied bombing raid. Bonhoeffer was transferred several more times, and was eventually taken to a detention camp at Schönberg on April 5, 1945. That day, Hitler decided that none of the remaining Abwehr group would live.

On April 8 Bonhoeffer conducted a service for his fellow prisoners. He chose as his texts Isaiah 53:5 ("With his stripes we are healed") and Peter 1:3 ("Blessed be the God and Father of our Lord Jesus Christ, which according to his abundant mercy hath begotten us again unto a lively hope by the resurrection of Jesus Christ from the dead"). As he came to the end of his message, the door was flung open and Bonhoeffer was ordered to collect his belongings. An English army officer who was present relayed Bonhoeffer's final greeting to Bishop Bell: ". . . This is the end, but for me, it is the beginning."

Bonhoeffer was taken to the Flossenburg concentration camp and sentenced to death after an all-night court-martial. The prison doctor saw him kneel in prayer shortly after the sentence was pronounced. The next morning, when he was taken to the scaffold, he knelt to pray once more. Then, courageously, he climbed the steps to the gallows, and at thirty-nine years of age Dietrich Bonhoeffer, a noble and dedicated disciple of Jesus Christ, was hanged.

There was no funeral. No gravestone marks the final resting place of this brilliant but humble theologian. His ashes were scattered to the winds—but the Nazis could not obliterate the memory or impact of this man.

Tertullian, a Roman converted to Christianity in A.D. 192, said, "The blood of the martyrs is the seed of the Church." Originally the word *martyr* meant "witness." This Bonhoeffer was, and his message is as relevant today as it was in Nazi Germany. His words bid us be dedicated witnesses in today's confusingly violent and needy world.

In compiling this anthology of Dietrich Bonhoeffer's writings, it has been my hope that those who are familiar with his works will find a further blessing in these excerpts. Those who are unacquainted with Bonhoeffer's thought-provoking and challenging words will find in this collection a rich encounter with a man who lived and died triumphantly, experiencing costly grace and close communion with his Lord and Savior.

JOAN WINMILL BROWN

Created in His Image

YAHWEH SHAPES MAN with his own hands. This expresses two things. First, the bodily nearness of the Creator to the creature, that it is really he who makes me—man—with his own hands; his concern, his thought for me, his design for me, his nearness to me. And secondly there is his authority, the absolute superiority in which he shapes and creates me, in which I am his creature; the fatherliness in which he creates me and in which I worship him. That is God himself, to whom the whole Bible testifies.

The man whom God has created in his image, that is in freedom, is the man who is formed out of earth. Darwin and Feuerbach themselves could not speak any more strongly. Man's origin is in a piece of earth. His bond with the earth belongs to his essential being. The "earth is his mother"; he comes out of her womb. Of course, the ground from which man is taken is still not the cursed but the blessed ground. It is God's earth out of which man is taken. From it he has his *body*. His body belongs to his essential being. Man's body is not his prison, his shell, his exterior, but man himself. Man does not "have" a body; he does not "have" a soul; rather, he "is" body and soul. Man in the beginning is really his body. He is one. He is his body, as Christ is completely his body, as the Church is the body of Christ. The man who renounces his body renounces his existence before God the Creator. The essential point of human existence is its bond with mother earth, its being as body. Man has his existence as existence on earth; he does not come to the earthly world from above, driven and enslaved by a cruel fate. He comes out of the earth in which he slept and was dead; he is called out by the Word of God the Almighty, in himself a piece of earth, but earth called into human being by God. "Awake, thou that sleepest, and arise from the dead, and Christ shall shine upon thee."[1] Michelangelo also meant this. Adam resting on the newly created ground is so closely and intimately bound up with the ground on which he lies that he himself, in his still dreaming existence, is strange and marvellous to the highest degree—but just the same he is a piece of earth. Surely, it is in this full devotion to the blessed ground of creation's earth that the complete glory of the first man becomes visible. And in this resting on the ground, in this deep sleep of creation, man experiences life through bodily contact with the finger of God—the same hand that has made man touches him tenderly as from afar and awakens him to life. God's hand does not hold man in its embrace any longer, but it sets him free, and its creative power becomes the demanding love of the Creator towards the creature. The hand of God portrayed by the picture in the Sistine Chapel reveals more wisdom about the creation than many a deep speculation.

[1]Ephesians 5:14

...And God breathed into his nostrils the breath of life; and man became a living being.

Here body and life enter into one another totally. God breathes his Spirit into the body of man. And this Spirit is life and makes man alive. God creates other life through his Word; where man is concerned he gives of his life, of his Spirit. Man as man does not live without God's Spirit. To live *as man* means to live as body in Spirit. Escape from the body is escape from being man and escape from the spirit as well. Body is the existence-form of spirit, as spirit is the existence-form of body. All this can be said only of man, for only in man do we know of body and spirit. The human body is distinguished from all non-human bodies by being the existence-form of God's Spirit on earth, as it is wholly undifferentiated from all other life by being of this earth. The human body really only lives by God's Spirit; this is indeed its essential nature. God glorifies himself in the body: in this specific form of the human body. For this reason God enters into the body again where the original in its created being has been destroyed. He enters it in Jesus Christ. He enters into it where it is broken, in the form of the sacrament of the body and of the blood. The body and blood of the Lord's Supper are the new realities of creation of the promise for the fallen Adam. Adam is created as body, and therefore he is also redeemed as body, in Jesus Christ and in the Sacrament.

Man thus created is man as the image of God. He is the image of God not in spite of but just because of his bodiliness. For in his bodiliness he is related to the earth and to other bodies, he is there for others, he is dependent upon others. In his bodiliness he finds his brother and the earth. As such a creature man of earth and spirit is in the likeness of his Creator, God.

The Kingdom of God

...GOD IS BEING increasingly pushed out of a world that has come of age, out of the spheres of our knowledge and life, and that since Kant he has been relegated to a realm beyond the world of experience. Theology has on the one hand resisted this development with apologetics, and has taken up arms—in vain—against Darwinism, etc. On the other hand, it has accommodated itself to the development by restricting God to the so-called ultimate questions as a *deus ex machina*; that means that he becomes the answer to life's problems, and the solution of its needs and conflicts. So if anyone has no such difficulties, or if he refuses to go into these things, to allow others to pity him, then either he cannot be open to God; or else he must be shown that he is, in fact, deeply involved in such problems, needs, and conflicts, without admitting or knowing it. If that can be done—and existentialist philosophy and psychotherapy have worked out some quite ingenious methods in that direction—then this man can now be claimed for God, and methodism can celebrate its triumph. But if he cannot be brought to see and admit that his happiness is really an evil, his health sickness, and his vigour despair, the theologian is at his wits' end. It's a case of having to do either with a hardened sinner of a particularly ugly type, or with a man of 'bourgeois complacency', and the one is as far from salvation as the other.

You see, that is the attitude that I am contending against. When Jesus blessed sinners, they were real sinners, but Jesus did not make everyone a sinner first. He called them away from their sin, not into their sin. It is true that encounter with Jesus meant the reversal of all human values. So it was in the conversion of Paul, though in his case the encounter with Jesus preceded the realization of sin. It is true that Jesus cared about people on the fringe of human society, such as harlots and tax-collectors, but never about them alone, for he sought to care about man as such. Never did he question a man's health, vigour, or happiness, regarded in themselves, or regard them as evil fruits; else why should he heal the sick and restore strength to the weak? Jesus claims for himself and the Kingdom of God the whole of human life in all its manifestations.

The Strength of God

THE DISPLACEMENT OF GOD from the world, and from the public part of human life, led to the attempt to keep his place secure at least in the sphere of the 'personal', the 'inner', and the 'private'. And as every man still has a private sphere somewhere, that is where he was thought to be the most vulnerable. The secrets known to a man's valet—that is, to put it crudely, the range of his intimate life, from prayer to his sexual life—have become the hunting-ground of modern pastoral workers. In that way they resemble (though with quite different intentions) the dirtiest gutter journalists—do you remember the *Wahrheit* and the *Glocke*,[1] which made public the most intimate

---

[1] Berlin papers from the Weimar period.

details about prominent people? In the one case it's social, financial, or political blackmail and in the other, religious blackmail. Forgive me, but I can't put it more mildly.

From the sociological point of view this is a revolution from below, a revolt of inferiority. Just as the vulgar mind isn't satisfied till it has seen some highly placed personage 'in his bath', or in other embarrassing situations, so it is here. There is a kind of evil satisfaction in knowing that everyone has his failings and weak spots. In my contacts with the 'outcasts' of society, its 'pariahs', I've noticed repeatedly that mistrust is the dominant motive in their judgment of other people. Every action, even the most unselfish, of a person of high repute is suspected from the outset. These 'outcasts' are to be found in all grades of society. In a flower-garden they grub around only for the dung on which the flowers grow. The more isolated a man's life, the more easily he falls a victim to this attitude.

There is also a parallel isolation among the clergy, in what one might call the 'clerical' sniffing-around-after-people's-sins in order to catch them out. It's as if you couldn't know a fine house till you had found a cobweb in the furthest cellar, or as if you couldn't adequately appreciate a good play till you had seen how the actors behave off-stage. It's the same kind of thing that you find in the novels of the last fifty years, which do not think they have depicted their characters properly till they have described them in their marriage-bed, or in films where undressing scenes are thought necessary. Anything clothed, veiled, pure, and chaste is presumed to be deceitful, disguised, and impure; people here simply show their own impurity. A basic anti-social attitude of mistrust and suspicion is the revolt of inferiority.

Regarded theologically, the error is twofold. First, it is thought that a man can be addressed as a sinner only after his weaknesses and meannesses have been spied out. Secondly, it is thought that a man's essential nature consists of his inmost and most intimate background; that is defined as his 'inner life', and it is precisely in those secret human places that God is to have his domain!

... The Bible does not recognize our distinction between the outward and the inward. Why should it? It is always concerned with *anthrōpos teleios,* the *whole* man, even where, as in the Sermon on the Mount, the decalogue is pressed home to refer to 'inward disposition'. That a good 'disposition' can take the place of total goodness is quite unbiblical. The discovery of the so-called inner life dates from the Renaissance, probably from Petrarch. The 'heart' in the biblical sense is not the inner life, but the whole man in relation to God. But as a man lives just as much from 'outwards' to 'inwards' as from 'inwards' to 'outwards', the view that his essential nature can be understood only from his intimate spiritual background is wholly erroneous.

I therefore want to start from the premise that God shouldn't be smuggled into some last secret place, but that we should frankly recognize that the world, and people, have come of age, that we shouldn't run man down in his worldliness, but confront him with God at his strongest point, that we should give up all our clerical tricks, and not regard psychotherapy and existentialist philosophy as God's pioneers. The importunity of all these people is far too unaristocratic for the Word of God to ally itself with them. The Word of God is far removed from this revolt of mistrust, this revolt from below. On the contrary, it reigns.

God's Faithfulness

...THERE IS HARDLY ANYTHING that can make one happier than to feel that one counts for something with other people. What matters here is not numbers, but intensity. In the long run, human relationships are the most important thing in life; the modern 'efficient' man can do nothing to change this, nor can the demigods and lunatics who know nothing about human relationships. God uses us in his dealings with others.

God's Blessing

...IN THE OLD TESTAMENT—e.g. among the patriarchs— there's a concern not for fortune, but for God's blessing, which includes in itself all earthly good. In that blessing the whole of the earthly life is claimed for God, and it includes all his promises. It would be natural to suppose that, as usual, the New Testament spiritualizes the teaching of the Old Testament here, and therefore to regard the Old Testament blessing as superseded in the New. But is it an accident that sickness and death are mentioned in connection with the misuse of the Lord's Supper ('The cup of blessing', I Cor. 10:16; 11:30), that Jesus restored people's health, and that while his disciples were with him they 'lacked nothing'? Now, is it right to set the Old

Testament blessing against the cross? That is what Kierkegaard did. That makes the cross, or at least suffering, an abstract principle; and that is just what gives rise to an unhealthy methodism, which deprives suffering of its element of contingency as a divine ordinance. It's true that in the Old Testament the person who receives the blessing has to endure a great deal of suffering (e.g. Abraham, Isaac, Jacob, and Joseph), but this never leads to the idea that fortune and suffering, blessing and cross are mutually exclusive and contradictory—nor does it in the New Testament. Indeed, the only difference between the Old and New Testaments in this respect is that in the Old the blessing includes the cross, and in the New the cross includes the blessing.

To turn to a different point: not only action, but also suffering is a way to freedom. In suffering, the deliverance consists in our being allowed to put the matter out of our own hands into God's hands. In this sense death is the crowning of human freedom. Whether the human deed is a matter of faith or not depends on whether we understand our suffering as an extension of our action and a completion of freedom. I think that is very important and very comforting.

The Commandment of God

EITHER GOD DOES NOT SPEAK at all or else He speaks to us as definitely as He spoke to Abraham and Jacob and Moses and as definitely as in Jesus Christ He spoke to the disciples and through His apostles to the Gentiles. Does this mean that at every moment of our lives we may be informed of the commandment of God by some special direct divine inspiration, or that at every moment, in an unmistakable and unequivocal manner, God causes what Karl Heim calls the 'accent of eternity' to rest on a particular action which He wills? No, it does not mean that, for the concreteness of the divine commandment consists in its historicity; it confronts us in a historical form. Does this mean, then, that we are utterly lacking in certainty in the face of the extremely varying claims of the historical powers, and that, so far as the commandment of God is concerned, we are groping in the darkness? No, the reason why it does not mean this is that God makes His commandment heard in a definite historical form. We cannot now escape the question where and in what historical form God makes His commandment known. For the sake of simplicity and clarity, and even at the risk of a direct misunderstanding, we will begin by answering this question in the form of a thesis. God's commandment, which is manifested in Jesus Christ, comes to us in the Church, in the family, in labour and in government.

It is a necessary premise which must never be lost sight of, even though for the time being it may not be fully intelligible, that the commandment of God is and always remains the commandment of God which is made manifest in Jesus Christ. There is no other commandment of God than that which is revealed by Him and which is manifested according to His will in Jesus Christ.

This means that the commandment of God does not spring from the created world. It comes down from above. It does not arise from the factual claim on men of earthly powers and laws, from the claim of the instinct of self-preservation or from the claim of hunger, sex or political force. It stands beyond all these as a demand, a precept and judgement. The commandment of God establishes on earth an inviolable superiority and inferiority which are independent of the factual relations of power and weakness. In establishing this superiority it confers that warrant for ethical discourse of which we have already spoken, or, more comprehensively, it confers the warrant to proclaim the divine commandment.

Christians and Pagans

1

Men go to God when they are sore bestead,
Pray to him for succour, for his peace, for bread,
For mercy for them sick, sinning, or dead;
All men do so, Christian and unbelieving.

2

Men go to God when he is sore bestead,
Find him poor and scorned, without shelter or bread,
Whelmed under weight of the wicked, the weak,
    the dead;
Christians stand by God in his hour of grieving.

3

God goes to every man when sore bestead,
Feeds body and spirit with his bread;
For Christians, pagans alike he hangs dead,
And both alike forgiving.

God's Will

...THE WILL OF GOD is not a system of rules which is established from the outset; it is something new and different in each different situation in life, and for this reason a man must ever anew examine what the will of God may be. The heart, the understanding, observation and experience must all collaborate in this task. It is no longer a matter of a man's own knowledge of good and evil, but solely of the living will of God; our knowledge of God's will is not something over which we ourselves dispose, but it depends solely upon the grace of God, and this grace is and requires to be new every morning. That is why this proving or examining of the will of God is so serious a matter. The voice of the heart is not to be confused with the will of God, nor is any kind of inspiration or any general principle, for the will of God discloses itself ever anew only to him who proves it ever anew.

Access to God

...NOT EVERYTHING THAT HAPPENS is simply 'God's will'; yet in the last resort nothing happens 'without God's will' (Matt. 10:29), i.e. through every event, however unto-

Editor's note: Written in Tegel Prison to his friend Eberhard Bethge.

ward, there is access to God. When a man enters on a supremely happy marriage and has thanked God for it, it is a terrible blow to discover that the same God who established the marriage now demands of us a period of such great deprivation. In my experience nothing tortures us more than longing. Some people have been so violently shaken in their lives from their earliest days that they cannot now, so to speak, allow themselves any great longing or put up with a long period of tension, and they find compensation in short-lived pleasures that offer readier satisfaction. That is the fate of the proletarian classes, and it is the ruin of all intellectual fertility. It's not true to say that it is good for a man to have suffered heavy blows early and often in life; in most cases it breaks him. True, it hardens people for times like ours, but it also greatly helps to deaden them. When *we* are forcibly separated for any considerable time from those whom we love, we simply *cannot*, as most can, get some cheap substitute through other people—I don't mean because of moral considerations, but just because we are what we are. Substitutes repel us; we simply have to wait and wait; we have to suffer unspeakably from the separation, and feel the longing till it almost makes us ill. That is the only way, although it is a very painful one, in which we can preserve unimpaired our relationship with our loved ones. A few times in my life I've come to know what homesickness means. There is nothing more painful, and during these months in prison I've sometimes been terribly homesick. And as I expect you will have to go through the same kind of thing in the coming months, I wanted to write and tell you what I've learnt about it, in case it may be of some help to you. The first result of such longing is always a wish to neglect the ordinary daily routine in some way or other, and that means that our lives become disordered. I used to be tempted sometimes to stay in bed after six in the morning (it would have been perfectly possible), and to sleep on. Up to now I've always been able to force myself not to do this; I realized that it would have been the first stage of capitulation, and that worse would probably have followed. An outward and purely physical régime (exercises and a cold wash down in the morning) itself provides some support for one's inner discipline. Further, there is nothing worse in such times than to try to find a substitute for the irreplaceable. It just does not work, and it leads to still greater indiscipline, for the strength to overcome tension (such strength can come only from looking the longing straight in the face) is impaired, and endurance becomes even more unbearable...

Another point: I don't think it is good to talk to strangers about our condition; that always stirs up one's troubles—although we ought to be ready, when occasion arises, to listen to those of other people. Above all, we must never give way to self-pity. And on the Christian aspect of the matter, there are some lines that say

> ...that we remember what we would forget,
> that this poor earth is not our home.

That is indeed something essential, but it must come last of all. I believe that we ought so to love and trust God in our *lives*, and in all the good things that he sends us, that when the time comes (but not before!) we may go to him with love, trust, and joy. But, to put it plainly, for a man in his wife's arms to be hankering after the other world is, in mild terms, a piece of bad taste, and not God's will. We ought to find and love God in what he actually gives us; if it pleases him to allow us to enjoy some overwhelming earthly happiness, we mustn't try to be more pious than God himself and allow our happiness to be corrupted by presumption and arrogance, and by unbridled religious fantasy which is never satisfied with what God gives. God will see to it that the man who finds him in his earthly happiness and thanks him for it does not lack reminder that earthly things are transient, that it is good for him to attune his heart to what is eternal, and that sooner or later there will be times when he can say in all sincerity, 'I wish I were home.' But everything has its time, and the main thing is that we keep step with God, and do not keep pressing on a few steps ahead—nor keep dawdling a step behind. It's presumptuous to want to have everything at once—matrimonial bliss, the cross, and the heavenly Jerusalem, where they neither marry nor are given in marriage. 'For everything there is a season' (Eccles. 3:1); everything has its time: 'a time to weep, and a time to laugh;...a time to embrace, and a time to refrain from embracing;...a time to rend, and a time to sew;...and God seeks again what is past.' I suspect that these last words mean that nothing that is past is lost, that God gathers up again with us our past, which belongs to us. So when we are seized by a longing for the past—and this may happen when we least expect it—we may be sure that it is only one of the many 'hours' that God is always holding ready for us. So we oughtn't to seek the past again by our own efforts, but only with God....

God Is No Stop-gap

...HOW WRONG IT IS to use God as a stop-gap for the incompleteness of our knowledge. If in fact the frontiers of knowledge are being pushed further and further back (and that is bound to be the case), then God is being pushed back with them, and is therefore continually in retreat. We are to find God in what we know, not in what we don't know; God wants us to realize his presence, not in unsolved problems but in those that are solved. That is true of the relationship between God and scientific knowledge, but it is also true of the wider human problems of death, suffering, and guilt. It is now possible to find, even for these questions, human answers that take no account whatever of God. In point of fact, people deal with these questions without God (it has always been so), and it is simply not true to say that only Christianity has the answers to them. As to the idea of 'solving' problems, it may be that the Christian answers are just as unconvincing—or convincing—as any others. Here again, God is no stop-gap; he must be recognized at the centre of life, not when we are at the end of our resources; it is his will to be recognized in life, and not only when death comes; in health and vigour, and not only in suffering; in our activities, and not only in sin. The ground for this lies in the revelation of God in Jesus Christ. He is the centre of life, and he certainly didn't 'come' to answer our unsolved problems. From the centre of life certain questions, and their answers, are seen to be wholly irrelevant (I'm thinking of the judgement pronounced on Job's friends). In Christ there are no 'Christian problems'. . .

The Name of Jesus Christ

. . .IT IS ONLY WHEN ONE KNOWS the unutterability of the name of God that one can utter the name of Jesus Christ; it is only when one loves life and the earth so much that without them everything seems to be over that one may believe in the resurrection and a new world; it is only when one submits to God's law that one may speak of grace; and it is only when God's wrath and vengeance are hanging as grim realities over the heads of one's enemies that something of what it means to love and forgive them can touch our hearts....

The Incarnate One

IF JESUS CHRIST IS TO BE DESCRIBED as God, we may not speak of this divine being, nor of his omnipotence, nor his omniscience; but we must speak of this weak man among sinners, of his manger and his cross. If we are to deal with the deity of Jesus, we must speak of his weakness. In christology, one looks at the whole historical man Jesus and says of him, that he is God. One does not first look at a human nature and then beyond it to a divine nature, but one has to do with the one man Jesus Christ, who is wholly God.

The accounts of the birth and of the baptism of Jesus stand side by side. In the birth story, we are directed totally towards Jesus himself. In the story of the baptism, we are directed towards the Holy Spirit who comes from above. The reason why we find it difficult to take the two stories together is because of the doctrine of the two natures. The two stories are not teaching two natures. If we put this doctrine aside, we see that the one story concerns the being of the Word of God in Jesus, while the other concerns the coming of the Word of God upon Jesus. The child in the manger is wholly God: note Luther's christology in the Christmas hymns. The call at the baptism is confirmation of the first happening, there is no adoptionism in it. The manger directs our attention to the man, who is God; the baptism directs our attention, as we look at Jesus, to the God who calls.

If we speak of Jesus Christ as God, we may not say of him that he is the representative of an idea of God, which possesses the characteristics of omniscience and omnipotence (there is no such thing as this abstract divine nature!); rather, we must speak of his weakness, his manger, his cross. This man is no abstract God.

Strictly speaking we should not talk of the incarnation, but of the incarnate one. The former interest arises out of the question, 'How?' The question, 'How?', for example, underlies the hypothesis of the virgin birth. Both historically and dogmatically it can be questioned. The biblical witness is ambiguous. If the biblical witness gave clear evidence of the fact, then the dogmatic obscurity might not have been so important. The doctrine of the virgin birth is meant to express the incarnation of God, not only the fact of the incarnate one. But does it not fail at the decisive point of the incarnation, namely that in it Jesus has not become man just like us? The question remains open, as and because it is already open in the Bible.

The incarnate one is the glorified God: 'The Word was made flesh and we beheld his glory'. God glorifies himself in man. That is the ultimate secret of the Trinity. The humanity is taken up into the Trinity. Not from all eternity, but 'from now on even unto eternity'; the trinitarian God is seen as the incarnate one. The glorification of God in the flesh is now at the same time, the glorification of man, who shall have life through eternity with the trinitarian God. This does not mean that we should see the incarnation of God as God's judgement on man. God remains the incarnate one even in the Last Judgement. The incarnation is the message of the glorification of God, who sees his honour in becoming man. It must be noted that the incarnation is first and foremost true revelation, of the Creator in the creature, and not veiled revelation. Jesus Christ is the unveiled image of God.

The incarnation of God may not be thought of as derived from an idea of God, in which something of humanity already belongs to the idea of God—as in Hegel. Here we speak of the biblical witness, 'We saw his glory'. If the incarnation is thus spoken of as the glorification of God, it is not permissible to slip in once again a speculative idea of God, which derives the incarnation from the necessity of an idea of God. A speculative basis for the doctrine of the incarnation in an idea of God would change the free relationship between Creator and creature into a logical necessity. The incarnation is contingent. God binds himself freely to the creature and freely glorifies himself in the incarnate one.

Why does that sound strange and improbable? Because the revelation of the incarnation in Jesus Christ is not visibly a glorification of God. Because this incarnate one is also the crucified.

The Body of Jesus Christ

GOD WAS MADE MAN, and while that means that he took upon him our entire human nature with all its infirmity, sinfulness and corruption, the whole of apostate humanity, it does not mean that he took upon him the man Jesus. Unless we draw this distinction we shall misunderstand the whole message of the gospel. The Body of Jesus Christ, in which we are taken up with the whole human race, has now become the ground of our salvation.

It is *sinful* flesh that he bears, though he was himself without sin (II Cor. 5:21; Heb. 4:15). In his human body he takes all flesh upon himself. "Surely he hath borne our griefs, and carried our sorrows." It is solely in virtue of the Incarnation that Jesus was able to heal the diseases and pains of human nature, because he bore upon his own body all these ills (Matt. 8:15–17). "He was wounded for our transgressions, he was bruised for our iniquities." He bore our sins, and was able to forgive them because he had "taken up" our sinful flesh in his Body. Similarly, Jesus received sinners and took them to himself (Luke 15:2) because he bore them in his own body. With the coming of Christ the "acceptable (δεκτόν) year of the Lord" had dawned (Luke 4:19).

. . . The earthly body of Jesus underwent crucifixion and death. In that death the new humanity undergoes crucifixion and death. Jesus Christ had taken upon him not a man, but the human "form," sinful flesh, human "nature," so that all whom he bore suffer and die with him. It is all our infirmities and all our sin that he bears to the cross. It is *we* who are crucified with him, and we who die with him. True, his earthly body undergoes death, but only to rise again as an incorruptible, glorious body. It is the same body—the tomb was empty—and yet it is a new body. And so as he dies, Jesus bears the human race, and carries it onward to resurrection. Thus, too, he bears for ever in his glorified body the humanity which he had taken upon him on earth.

How then do we come to participate in the Body of Christ, who did all this for us? It is certain that there can be no fellowship or communion with him except through his Body. For only through that Body can we find acceptance and salvation. The answer is, through the two sacraments of his Body, baptism and the Lord's Supper. Note how in recording the incident of the water and blood which issued from the side of the crucified body of Christ, St John refers unmistakably to the elements of the two sacraments (John 19:34, 35). St Paul corroborates this when he rivets our membership of the Body of Christ exclusively to the two sacraments.[1] The sacraments begin and end in the Body of Christ, and it is only the presence of that Body which makes them what they are. The word of preaching is insufficient to make us members of Christ's Body; the sacraments also have to be added. Baptism incorporates us into the unity of the Body of Christ, and the Lord's Supper fosters and sustains our fellowship and communion (κοινωνία) in that Body. Baptism makes us members of the Body of Christ. We are "baptized into" Christ (Gal. 3:27; Rom. 6:3); we are "baptized into one body" (I Cor. 12:13). Our death in baptism conveys the gift of the Holy Spirit, and gains the redemption which Christ wrought for us in his body. The communion of the body of Christ, which we receive as the disciples received it in the early days, is the sign and pledge that we are "with Christ" and "in Christ," and that he is "in us." Rightly understood, the doctrine of the Body is the clue to the meaning of these expressions.

[1] Eph. 3:6 likewise embraces the whole gift of salvation—the Word, Baptism, and the Lord's Supper.

The Lordship of Jesus Christ

Jesus Christ, the eternal Son with the Father for all eternity: this means that no created thing can be conceived and essentially understood without reference to Christ, the Mediator of creation. All things were created by Him and for Him, and have their existence only in Him (Col. 1:15ff.). It is vain to seek to know God's will for created things without reference to Christ. Jesus Christ, the incarnate God: this means that God has taken upon himself bodily all human being; it means that henceforward divine being cannot be found otherwise than in human form; it means that in Jesus Christ man is made free to be really man before God. The 'Christian' element is not now something which lies beyond the human element; it requires to be in the midst of the human element. The 'Christian' element is not an end in itself, but it consists in man's being entitled and obliged to live as man before God. In the incarnation God makes Himself known as Him who wishes to exist not for Himself but 'for us'. Consequently, in view of the incarnation of God, to live as man before God can mean only to exist not for oneself but for God and for other men.

Jesus Christ, the crucified Reconciler: this means in the first place that the whole world has become godless by its rejection of Jesus Christ and that no effort of its own can rid it of this curse. The reality of the world has been marked once and for all by the cross of Christ, but the cross of Christ is the cross of the reconciliation of the world with God, and for this reason the godless world bears at the same time the mark of reconciliation as the free ordinance of God. The cross of atonement is the setting free for life before God in the midst of the godless world; it is the setting free for life in genuine worldliness. The proclamation of the cross of the atonement is a setting free because it leaves behind it the vain attempts to deify the world and because it has overcome the disunions, tensions and conflicts between the 'Christian' element and the 'secular' element and calls for simple life and action in the belief that the reconciliation of the world with God has been accomplished.

. . . *Jesus Christ, the risen and ascended Lord:* this means that Jesus Christ has overcome sin and death and that He is the living Lord to whom all power is given in heaven and on earth. All the powers of the world are made subject to Him and must serve Him, each in its own way. The lordship of Jesus Christ is not the rule of a foreign power; it is the lordship of the Creator, Reconciler and Redeemer, the lordship of Him through whom and for whom all created beings exist, of Him in whom indeed all created beings alone find their origin, their goal and their essence. Jesus Christ imposes no alien law upon creation; but at the same time He does not tolerate any 'autonomy' of creation in detachment from His commandments. The commandment of Jesus Christ, the living Lord, sets creation free for the fulfilment of the law which is its own, that is to say, the law which is inherent in it by virtue of its having its origin, its goal and its essence in Jesus Christ. The commandment of Jesus does not provide the basis for any kind of domination of the Church over the government, of the government over the family, or of culture over government or Church, or for any other relation of over-lordship which may be thought of in this connexion. The commandment of Jesus Christ does indeed rule over Church, family, culture and government; but it does so while at the same time setting each of these mandates free for the fulfilment of its own allotted functions. Jesus Christ's claim to lordship, which is proclaimed by the Church, means at the same time the emancipation of family, culture and government for the realization of their own essential character which has its foundation in Christ.[1] The liberation which results from the proclamation of the lordship of Christ alone renders possible that relation of the divine mandates 'with', 'for' and 'against' one another....

[1] The antinomy of heteronomy and autonomy is here resolved in a higher unity which we may call Christonomy.

The Light of His Presence

ALL THAT WE MAY RIGHTLY EXPECT from God, and ask him for, is to be found in Jesus Christ. The God of Jesus Christ has nothing to do with what God, as we imagine him, could do and ought to do. If we are to learn what God promises, and what he fulfils, we must persevere in quiet meditation on the life, sayings, deeds, sufferings, and death of Jesus. It is certain that we may always live close to God and in the light of his presence, and that such living is an entirely new life for us; that nothing is then impossible for us, because all things are possible with God; that no earthly power can touch us without his will, and that danger and distress can only drive us closer to him. It is certain that we can claim nothing for ourselves, and may yet pray for everything; it is certain that our joy is hidden in suffering, and our life in death; it is certain that in all this we are in a fellowship that sustains us. In Jesus God has said Yes and Amen to it all, and that Yes and Amen is the firm ground on which we stand.

In these turbulent times we repeatedly lose sight of what really makes life worth living. We think that, because this or that person is living, it makes sense for us to live too. But the truth is that if this earth was good enough for the man Jesus Christ, if such a man as Jesus lived, then, and only then, has life a meaning for us. If Jesus had not lived, then our life would be meaningless, in spite of all the other people whom we know and honour and love. Perhaps we now sometimes forget the meaning and purpose of our profession. But isn't this the simplest way of putting it? The unbiblical idea of 'meaning' is indeed only a translation of what the Bible calls 'promise'.

'I Am the Life'

JESUS CHRIST SAID of Himself: 'I am the life' (John 14:6 and 11:25), and this claim, and the reality which it contains cannot be disregarded by any Christian thinking, or indeed by any philosophical thinking at all. This self-affirmation of Jesus is a declaration that any attempt to express the essence of life simply as life is foredoomed to failure and has indeed already failed. So long as we live, so long as we do not know the boundary of life, death, how can we possibly say what life is in itself? We can only live life; we cannot define it. Jesus's saying binds every thought of life to His person. 'I am the life.' No question about life can go further back than this 'I am'. The question of what is life gives place to the answer who is life. Life is not a thing, an entity or concept; it is a person, a particular and unique person, and it is this particular and unique person, not in respect of what this person has in common with other persons, but in the I of this person; it is the I of Jesus. Jesus sets this I in sharp contrast with all the thoughts, concepts and ways which claim to constitute the essence of life. He does not say 'I have the life' but 'I am the life.' Consequently life can never again be separated from the I, the person, of Jesus. In proclaiming this, Jesus does not merely say that He is life, in other words simply some metaphysical spirit which might possibly light upon me as well as upon others; He says that He is precisely my life, our life; St Paul describes this state of affairs very accurately, though also very paradoxically, in the words 'To me to live is Christ' (Phil. 1:21) and 'Christ who is our life' (Col. 3:4). My life is outside myself, outside the range of my disposal; my life is another than myself; it is Jesus Christ. This is not intended figuratively, as conveying that my life would not be worth living without this other, or that Christ invests my life with a particular quality or a particular value while allowing it to retain its own independent existence, but my life itself is Jesus Christ. That is true of my life, and it is true of all created things. 'In all things that were made—He was the life' (John 1:4).[1]

'I am the life.' This is the word, the revelation, the proclamation of Jesus Christ. Our life is outside ourselves and in Jesus Christ; this is not at all a conclusion which we derive from our knowledge of ourselves; it is a claim which comes to us from without, a claim which we may either believe or contradict. This word is addressed to us, and when we hear it we recognize that we have fallen away from life, from our life, and that we are living in contradiction to life, to our life. In this saying of Jesus Christ, therefore, we hear the condemnation, the negation, of our life; for our life is not life; or, if it is life, it is life only by virtue of the fact that, even though in contradiction to it, we still live through the life which is called Jesus Christ, the origin, the essence and the goal of all life and of our life. This negation of our apostate life means that between it and the life which is Jesus Christ there stands the end, annihilation, death. This negation, the 'no' that we hear, itself brings us this death. But in bringing us death this 'no' becomes a mysterious 'yes', the affirmation of a new life, the life which is Jesus Christ. This is the life that we cannot give to ourselves, the life that comes to us entirely from without, entirely from beyond; and yet it is not a remote or alien life, of no concern to ourselves, but it

---

[1]*Cf:* Bultmann, *Das Evangelium des Johannes,* p.21ff.

is our own real daily life. This life lies hidden only behind the symbol of death, the symbol of negation.

We live now in tension between the negation and the affirmation. Our life can be spoken of now only in this relation to Jesus Christ. If we leave Him out of the reckoning, as the origin, the essence and the goal of life, of our life, if we fail to consider that we are creatures, reconciled and redeemed, then we shall achieve no more than mere biological and ideological abstractions. Our life is created, reconciled and redeemed; it finds in Jesus Christ its origin, its essence and its goal.. . .

Ecce Homo!

Ecce homo!—Behold the man! In Him the world was reconciled with God. It is not by its overthrowing but by its reconciliation that the world is subdued. It is not by ideals and programmes or by conscience, duty, responsibility and virtue that reality can be confronted and overcome, but simply and solely by the perfect love of God. Here again it is not by a general idea of love that this is achieved, but by the really *lived* love of God in Jesus Christ. This love of God does not withdraw from reality into noble souls secluded from the world. It experiences and suffers the reality of the world in all its hardness. The world exhausts its fury against the body of Christ. But, tormented, He forgives the world its sin. That is how the reconciliation is accomplished. *Ecce homo!*

The figure of the Reconciler, of the God-Man Jesus Christ, comes between God and the world and fills the centre of all history. In this figure the secret of the world is laid bare, and in this figure there is revealed the secret of

God. No abyss of evil can remain hidden from Him through whom the world is reconciled with God. But the abyss of the love of God encompasses even the most abysmal godlessness of the world. In a manner which passes all comprehension God reverses the judgement of justice and piety, declares Himself guilty towards the world, and thereby wipes out the world's guilt. God Himself sets out on the path of humiliation and atonement, and thereby absolves the world. God is willing to be guilty of our guilt. He takes upon Himself the punishment and the suffering which this guilt has brought on us. God Himself answers for godlessness, love for hatred, the saint for the sinner. Now there is no more godlessness, no more hatred, no more sin which God has not taken upon Himself, suffered for and expiated. Now there is no more reality, no more world, but it is reconciled with God and at peace. God did this in His dear Son Jesus Christ. *Ecce homo!*

...*Ecce homo!*—Behold the man sentenced by God, the figure of grief and pain. That is how the Reconciler of the world appears. The guilt of mankind has fallen upon Him. It casts Him into shame and death before God's judgement seat. This is the great price which God pays for reconciliation with the world. Only by God's executing judgement upon Himself can there be peace between Him and the world and between man and man. But the secret of this judgement, of this passion and death, is the love of God for the world and for man. What befell Christ befalls every man in Him. It is only as one who is sentenced by God that man can live before God. Only the crucified man is at peace with God. It is in the figure of the Crucified that man recognizes and discovers himself. To be taken up by God, to be executed on the cross and reconciled, that is the reality of manhood.

The Cross of Christ

...THE WHOLE STORY of death begins with Cain. Adam, preserved on the way to death and consumed with thirst for life, begets Cain, the murderer. The new thing about Cain, the son of Adam, is that as man *sicut deus* Cain himself lays violent hands on human life. The man who is not allowed to eat of the tree of life all the more greedily reaches out for the fruit of death, the destruction of life. Only the Creator can destroy life. Cain usurps this ultimate right of the Creator and becomes a murderer. Why does Cain murder? Out of hatred towards God. This hatred is great. Cain is great, he is greater than Adam, for his hatred is greater, and this means that his yearning for life is greater. The story of death stands under the mark of Cain.

Christ on the Cross, the murdered Son of God, is the end of the story of Cain, and thus the actual end of the story. This is the last desperate storming of the gate of paradise. And under the flaming sword under the Cross, mankind dies. But Christ lives. The stem of the Cross becomes the staff of life, and in the midst of the world life is set up anew upon the cursed ground. In the middle of the world the spring of life wells up on the wood of the Cross and those who thirst for life are called to this water, and those who have eaten of the wood of this life shall never hunger and thirst again. What a strange paradise is this hill of Golgotha, this Cross, this blood, this broken body! What a strange tree of life, this tree on which God himself must suffer and die—but it is in fact the Kingdom of Life and of the Resurrection given again by God in grace; it is the opened door of imperishable hope, of waiting and of patience. The tree of life, the Cross of Christ, the middle of the fallen and preserved world of God, for us that is the end of the story of paradise.

> He unlocks again the door
> Of paradise today:
> The angel guards the gate no more.
> To God our thanks we pay.

The Love of God

...CHRIST DIED FOR THE WORLD, and it is only in the midst of the world that Christ is Christ. Only unbelief can wish to give the world something less than Christ. Certainly it may have well-intentioned pedagogical motives for this course, but these motives always have a certain flavour of clerical exclusiveness. Such a course implies failure to take seriously the incarnation, the crucifixion and the bodily resurrection. It is a denial of the body of Christ.

If we now follow the New Testament in applying to the Church the concept of the body of Christ, this is not by any means intended primarily as representing the separation of the Church from the world. On the contrary, it is implicit in the New Testament statement concerning the incarnation of God in Christ that all men are taken up, enclosed and borne within the body of Christ and that this is just what the congregation of the faithful are to make known to the world by their words and by their lives. What is intended here is not separation from the world but the summoning of the world into the fellowship of this body of Christ, to which in truth it already belongs. This testimony of the Church is foreign to the world; the

Church herself, in bearing this testimony, finds herself to be foreign to the world. Yet even this is always only an ever-renewed consequence of that fellowship with the world which is given in the body of Christ. The Church is divided from the world solely by the fact that she affirms in faith the reality of God's acceptance of man, a reality which is the property of the whole world. By allowing this reality to take effect within herself, she testifies that it is effectual for the whole world.

The body of Jesus Christ, especially as it appears to us on the cross, shows to the eyes of faith the world in its sin, and how it is loved by God, no less than it shows the Church, as the congregation of those who acknowledge their sin and submit to the love of God.

Easter

EASTER? We're paying more attention to dying than to death. We're more concerned to get over the act of dying than to overcome death. Socrates mastered the art of dying; Christ overcame death as 'the last enemy' (I Cor. 15:26). There is a real difference between the two things; the one is within the scope of human possibilities, the other means resurrection. It's not from *ars moriendi,* the art of dying, but from the resurrection of Christ, that a new and purifying wind can blow through our present world. *Here* is the answer to δὸς μοὶ ποῦ στῶ καὶ κινήσω τὴν γῆν.[1] If a few people really believed that and acted on it in their daily lives, a great deal would be changed. To live in the light of the resurrection—that is what Easter means....

[1]'Give me somewhere to stand, and I will move the earth' (Archimedes).

The Glory of His Resurrection

IF WE ARE CONFORMED to his image in his Incarnation and crucifixion, we shall also share the glory of his resurrection. "We shall also bear the image of the heavenly" (I Cor. 15:49). "We shall be like him, for we shall see him even as he is" (I John 3:2). If we contemplate the image of the glorified Christ, we shall be made like unto it, just as by contemplating the image of Christ crucified we are conformed to his death. We shall be drawn into his image, and identified with his form, and become a reflection of him. That reflection of his glory will shine forth in us even in this life, even as we share his agony and bear his cross. Our life will then be a progress from knowledge to knowledge, from glory to glory, to an ever closer conformity with the image of the Son of God. "But we all, with unveiled face reflecting as a mirror the glory of the Lord, are transformed into the same image from glory to glory" (II Cor. 3:18).

This is what we mean when we speak of Christ dwelling in our hearts. His life on earth is not finished yet, for he continues to live in the lives of his followers. Indeed it is wrong to speak of the Christian life: we should speak rather of Christ living in us. "I live, and yet no longer I, but Christ liveth in me" (Gal. 2:20). Jesus Christ, incarnate, crucified and glorified, has entered my life and taken charge. "To me to live is Christ" (Phil. 1:21). And where Christ lives, there the Father also lives, and both Father and Son through the Holy Ghost. The Holy Trinity himself has made his dwelling in the Christian heart, filling his whole being, and transforming him into the divine image. Christ, incarnate, crucified and glorified is formed in every Christian soul, for all are members of his Body, the Church. The Church bears the human form, the form of Christ in his death and resurrection. The Church in the first place is his image, and through the Church all her members have been refashioned in his image too. In the Body of Christ we are become "like Christ."

His Ascension

SINCE THE ASCENSION, Christ's place on earth has been taken by his Body, the Church. The Church is the real presence of Christ. Once we have realized this truth we are well on the way to recovering an aspect of the Church's being which has been sadly neglected in the past. We should think of the Church not as an institution, but as a *person*, though of course a person in a unique sense.

The Church is One Man. All who are baptized are "one in Christ" (Gal. 3:28; Rom. 12:5; I Cor. 10:17). The Church is "Man," the "New Man" (καινός ἄνθρωπος). The Church is created as the new man through Christ's death on the cross. On the cross the enmity between Jew and Gentile was abolished, that enmity which rent the world in two, "that he might create in himself of the twain one new man, so making peace" (Eph. 2:15). The "new man" is one, not many. Beyond the confines of the Church, the new man, there is only the old humanity with all its divisions.

Challenge to Faith

IF CHRIST HAD PROVED HIMSELF by miracles, we would have believed in the visible *theophany* of deity, but that would not have been faith in Christ *pro me*. It would not have been inner conversion, but simply acknowledgement. Belief in miracles is no more than believing the evidence of one's eyes in visible Epiphany. When I acknowledge a miracle nothing happens to me. But faith is there when a man so surrenders himself to the humiliated God-Man that he bets his life on him, even when this seems against all sense. Faith is when the search for certainty out of visible evidence is given up. Then it is faith in God and not in the world. The only assurance which faith accepts is the Word itself, which comes to me through Christ.

Whoever seeks signs to establish his faith remains with himself. Nothing is changed. Whoever recognizes the Son through the stumbling block is a believer in the sense of the New Testament. He sees the Christ *pro nobis*, he is reconciled and become new. The stumbling block which the incognito presents and the ambiguous form of the Christ *pro nobis* pose at the same time the continuing challenge to faith. Yet, this challenge teaches us to pay attention to the Word (Isaiah 28:19). And from the Word comes faith.

The Word of God

WE LIVE BY RESPONDING to the word of God which is addressed to us in Jesus Christ. Since this word is addressed to our entire life, the response, too, can only be an entire one; it must be given with our entire life as it is realized in all our several actions. The life which confronts us in Jesus Christ, as a 'yes' and a 'no' to our life, requires the response of a life which assimilates and unites this 'yes' and this 'no'.

We give the name responsibility to this life in its aspect as a response to the life of Jesus Christ as the 'yes' and the 'no' to our life. This concept of responsibility is intended as referring to the concentrated totality and unity of the response to the reality which is given to us in Jesus Christ, as distinct from the partial responses which might arise, for example, from a consideration of utility or from particular principles. In the face of the life which confronts us in Jesus Christ these partial responses are not enough and nothing less can suffice than the entire and single response of our life. Responsibility means, therefore, that the totality of life is pledged and that our action becomes a matter of life and death.

In this way we invest the concept of responsibility with a fulness of meaning which it does not acquire in everyday usage, even when it is placed extremely high on the scale of ethical values, as it was, for example, by Bismarck and Max Weber. Even in the Bible we scarcely find such great prominence given to this concept, though when it does appear it displays quite decisive characteristics. Responsibility in the biblical sense is, in the first place, a verbal response given at the risk of a man's life to the question asked by another man with regard to the event of Christ (II Tim. 4:16; I Pet. 3:15; Phil. 1:7 and 17). I answer with words at the risk of my life for that which has taken place through Jesus Christ. I do not therefore answer primarily for myself, for my own action; I do not justify myself (II Cor. 12:19); I answer for Jesus Christ and thereby also indeed for the commission which has been encharged to me by Him (I Cor. 9:3). Job presumptuously desires to answer for his own ways before God (Job 13:15), and God's words to Job put an end to any such temerity: 'He that reproveth God, let him answer it. Then Job answered the Lord, and said, Behold, I am vile; what shall I answer thee? I will lay mine hand upon my mouth' (Job 40:2–4). We are continuing along the lines of the Bible if we say that in answering for Christ, for life, before men, and only thus, I am at the same time accepting responsibility for men before Christ; I stand for Christ before men and for men before Christ. The responsibility which I assume for Christ in speaking to men is also my responsibility for men in speaking to Christ. My answering to men for Christ is my answering to Christ for men, and only in this is it my answering for myself to God and to men. When I am called to account by men and by God I can answer only through the witness of Jesus Christ who interceded for God with men and for men with God. There is responsibility to God and for God, to men and for men; it is always responsibility for the sake of Jesus Christ, and in this alone it is responsibility for my own life. A man can answer for himself only in confessing Jesus Christ with his lips and with his life.

The Cause Is Urgent

THE KING STANDS at the door, and he may come in at any moment. Will you bow down and humbly receive him, or do you want him to destroy you in his wrath? Those who have ears to hear have heard all there is to hear. They cannot detain the messengers any longer, for they must be off to the next city. If, however, men refuse to hear, they have lost their chance, the time of grace is passed, and they have pronounced their own doom. "To-day if ye shall hear his voice, harden not your hearts" (Heb. 4:7). That is evangelical preaching. Is this ruthless speed? Nothing could be more ruthless than to make men think there is still plenty of time to mend their ways. To tell men that the cause is urgent, and that the kingdom of God is at hand is the most charitable and merciful act we can perform, the most joyous news we can bring. The messenger cannot wait and repeat it to every man in his own language. God's language is clear enough. It is not for the messenger to decide who will hear and who will not, for only God knows who is "worthy"; and those who are worthy will hear the Word when the disciple proclaims it. But woe to the city and woe to the house which rejects the messenger of Christ. They will incur a dreadful judgement; Sodom and Gomorrah, the cities of unchastity and perversion, will be judged more graciously than those cities of Israel who reject the word of Jesus. Vice and sin may be forgiven, according to the word of Jesus, but the man who rejects the word of salvation has thrown away his last chance. To refuse to believe in the gospel is the worst sin imaginable, and if that happens the messengers can do nothing but leave the place. They go because the Word cannot remain there. They must recognize in fear and amazement both the power and the weakness of the Word of God. But the disciples must not force any issue contrary to or beyond the word of Christ. Their commission is not a heroic struggle, a financial pursuit of a grand idea or a good cause. That is why they stay only where the Word stays, and if it is rejected they will be rejected with it, and shake off the dust from their feet as a sign of the curse which awaits that place. This curse will not harm the disciples, but the peace they brought returns to them. "This is a great consolation for ministers of the Church when they are troubled because their work seems void of success. You must not be depressed, for what others refuse will prove an even greater blessing for yourselves. To such the Lord says: 'They have scorned it, so keep it for yourselves'" (Bengel).

The Acceptance of Guilt

...JESUS IS NOT CONCERNED with the proclamation and realization of new ethical ideals; He is not concerned with Himself being good (Matt. 19:17); He is concerned solely with love for the real man, and for that reason He is able to enter into the fellowship of the guilt of men and to take the burden of their guilt upon Himself. Jesus does not desire to be regarded as the only perfect one at the expense of men; He does not desire to look down on mankind as the only guiltless one while mankind goes to its ruin under the weight of its guilt; He does not wish that some idea of a new man should triumph amid the wreckage of a humanity whose guilt has destroyed it. He does not wish to acquit Himself of the guilt under which men die. A love which left man alone in his guilt would not be love for the real man. As one who acts responsibly in the historical existence of men Jesus becomes guilty. It must be emphasized that it is solely His love which makes Him incur guilt. From His selfless love, from His freedom from sin, Jesus enters into the guilt of men and takes this guilt upon Himself. Freedom from sin and the question of guilt are inseparable in Him. It is as the one who is without sin that Jesus takes upon Himself the guilt of His brothers, and it is under the burden of this guilt that He shows Himself to be without sin. In this Jesus Christ, who is guilty without sin, lies the origin of every action of responsible deputyship. If it is responsible action, if it is action which is concerned solely and entirely with the other man, if it arises from selfless love for the real man who is our brother, then, precisely because this is so, it cannot wish to shun the fellowship of human guilt. Jesus took upon Himself the guilt of all men, and for that reason every man who acts responsibly becomes guilty. If any man tries to escape guilt in responsibility he detaches himself from the ultimate reality of human existence, and what is more he cuts himself off from the redeeming mystery of Christ's bearing guilt without sin and he has no share in the divine justification which lies upon this event. He sets his own personal innocence above his responsibility for men, and he is blind to the more irredeemable guilt which he incurs precisely in this; he is blind also to the fact that real innocence shows itself precisely in a man's entering into the fellowship of guilt for the sake of other men. Through Jesus Christ it becomes an essential part of responsible action that the man who is without sin loves selflessly and for that reason incurs guilt.

The Decision

THE POWER which men enjoy for a brief space on earth is not without the cognizance and the will of God. If we fall into the hands of men, and meet suffering and death from their violence, we are none the less certain that everything comes from God. The same God who sees no sparrow fall to the ground without his knowledge and will, allows nothing to happen, except it be good and profitable for his children and the cause for which they stand. We are in God's hands. Therefore, "Fear not."

The time is short. Eternity is long. It is the time of decision. Those who are true to the word and confession on earth will find Jesus Christ standing by their side in the hour of judgement. He will acknowledge them and come to their aid when the accuser demands his rights. All the world will be called to witness as Jesus pronounces our name before his heavenly Father. If we have been true to Jesus in this life, he will be true to us in eternity. But if we have been ashamed of our Lord and of his name, he will likewise be ashamed of us and deny us.

The final decision must be made while we are still on earth. The peace of Jesus is the cross. But the cross is the sword God wields on earth. It creates division. The son against the father, the daughter against her mother, the member of the house against the head—all this will happen in the name of God's kingdom and his peace. That is the work which Christ performs on earth. It is hardly surprising that the harbinger of God's love has been accused of hatred of the human race. Who has a right to speak thus of love for father and mother, for son and daughter, but the destroyer of all human life on the one hand, or the Creator of a new life on the other? Who dare lay such an exclusive claim to man's love and devotion, but the enemy of mankind on the one hand, and the Saviour of mankind on the other? Who but the devil, or Christ, the Prince of Peace, will carry the sword into men's houses? God's love for man is altogether different from the love of men for their own flesh and blood. God's love for man means the cross and the way of discipleship. But that cross and that way are both life and resurrection. "He that loseth his life for my sake shall find it." In this promise we hear the voice of him who holds the keys of death, the Son of God, who goes to the cross and the resurrection, and with him takes his own.

The Call of Jesus

IF CHRIST IS THE LIVING LORD of my life, my encounter with him discloses his word for me, and indeed I have no other means of knowing him, but through his plain word and command. You may of course object that our trouble is that we should like to know Christ and believe on him, but have no means of knowing his will. But such an objection only shows that our knowledge of him is neither genuine nor clear. To know Christ means to know him by his word as the Lord and Saviour of my life. But that knowledge includes a recognition of his plain word directed to me.

Suppose then we say finally that whereas the commandment the disciples received was plain and clear enough, *we* have to decide for ourselves which of his words applies to our particular case. That again is a complete misunderstanding of the situation of the disciples, and of our own situation too. The object of Jesus' command is always the same—to evoke wholehearted faith, to make us love God and our neighbour with all our heart and soul. This is the only unequivocal feature in his command. Every time we try to perform the commandment of Jesus in some other sense, it is another sign that we have misunderstood his word and are disobeying it. But this does not mean that we have no means whatever of ascertaining what he would have us do in any concrete situation. On the contrary, we are told quite clearly what we have to do every time we hear the word of Christ proclaimed; yet in such a way that we understand that there is no other way of fulfilling it, but by faith in Jesus Christ alone. Thus the gift Jesus gave to his disciples is just as available for us as it was for them. In fact it is even more readily available for us now that he has left the world, because we know that he is glorified, and because the Holy Spirit is with us.

It is therefore abundantly clear that we cannot play off the various accounts of the calling of the disciples against other parts of the gospel narrative. It is not a question of stepping into the shoes of the disciples, or of any other of the New Testament characters. The only constant factor throughout is the sameness of Christ and of his call then and now. His word is one and the same, whether it was addressed during his earthly life to the paralysed or the disciples, or whether it is speaking to us to-day. Here, as there, we receive the gracious summons to enter his kingdom and his glory. It is dangerous to ask whether we are to draw a parallel between ourselves and the disciples or ourselves and the paralytic. We may not compare ourselves to either. All we have to do is to hear the word and obey the will of Christ, in whatever part of the scripture testimony it is proclaimed. The scriptures do not present us with a series of Christian types to be imitated according to choice: they preach to us in every situation the one Jesus Christ. To him alone must I listen. He is everywhere one and the same.

To the question—where to-day do we hear the call of Jesus to discipleship, there is no other answer than this: Hear the Word, receive the Sacrament; in it hear him himself, and you will hear his call.

The Christian Life

JESUS ASKED IN GETHSEMANE, 'Could you not watch with me one hour?' That is a reversal of what the religious man expects from God. Man is summoned to share in God's sufferings at the hands of a godless world.

He must therefore really live in the godless world, without attempting to gloss over or explain its ungodliness in some religious way or other. He must live a 'secular' life, and thereby share in God's sufferings. He *may* live a 'secular' life (as one who has been freed from false religious obligations and inhibitions). To be a Christian does not mean to be religious in a particular way, to make something of oneself (a sinner, a penitent, or a saint) on the basis of some method or other, but to be a man— not a type of man, but the man that Christ creates in us. It is not the religious act that makes the Christian, but participation in the sufferings of God in the secular life. That is *metanoia:* not in the first place thinking about one's own needs, problems, sins, and fears, but allowing oneself to be caught up into the way of Jesus Christ, into the messianic event, thus fulfilling Isa. 53. Therefore 'believe in the gospel', or, in the words of John the Baptist, 'Behold, the Lamb of God, who takes away the sin of the world' (John 1:29). (By the way, Jeremias has recently asserted that the Aramaic word for 'lamb' may also be translated 'servant'; very appropriate in view of Isa. 53!)

This being caught up into the messianic sufferings of God in Jesus Christ takes a variety of forms in the New Testament. It appears in the call to discipleship, in Jesus' table-fellowship with sinners, in 'conversions' in the narrower sense of the word (e.g. Zacchaeus), in the act of the woman who was a sinner (Luke 7)—an act that she performed without any confession of sin, in the healing of the sick (Matt. 8:17; see above), in Jesus' acceptance of children. The shepherds, like the wise men from the East, stand at the crib, not as 'converted sinners', but simply because they are drawn to the crib by the star just as they are. The centurion of Capernaum (who makes no confession of sin) is held up as a model of faith (cf. Jairus). Jesus 'loved' the rich young man. The eunuch (Acts 8) and Cornelius (Acts 10) are not standing at the edge of an abyss. Nathaniel is 'an Israelite indeed, in whom there is no guile' (John 1:47). Finally, Joseph of Arimathea and the women at the tomb. The only thing that is common to all these is their sharing in the suffering of God in Christ. That is their 'faith'. There is nothing of religious method here. The 'religious act' is always something partial; 'faith' is something whole, involving the whole of one's life. Jesus calls men, not to a new religion, but to life.

Christ Our Hope

THE IMPORTANCE OF ILLUSION to one's life should certainly not be underestimated; but for a Christian there must be hope based on a firm foundation. And if even illusion has so much power in people's lives that it can keep life moving, how great a power there is in a hope that is based on certainty, and how invincible a life with such a hope is. 'Christ our hope'—this Pauline formula is the strength of our lives.

The Imparting of Grace

CHRIST COMES INDEED, and opens up His own way, no matter whether man is ready beforehand or not. No one can hinder His coming, but we can resist His coming in mercy. There are conditions of the heart, of life and of the world which impede the reception of grace in a special way, namely, by rendering faith infinitely difficult. We say that they impede it and render it difficult, but not that they make it impossible. And we are well aware also that even the levelling of the way and the removal of the obstacles cannot compel the imparting of grace. The merciful coming of Christ must still 'break the gates of brass and cut the bars of iron' (Ps. 107:16); grace must in the end itself prepare and make level its own way and grace alone must ever anew render possible the impossible. But all this does not release us from our obligation to prepare the way for the coming of grace, and to remove whatever obstructs it and makes it difficult. The state in which grace finds us is not a matter of indifference, even though it is always by grace alone that grace comes to us. We may, among other things, make it difficult for ourselves to attain to faith. For him who is cast into utter shame, desolation, poverty and helplessness, it is difficult to have faith in the justice and goodness of God. For him whose life has become a prey to disorder and indiscipline, it will be difficult to hear the commandments of God in faith. It is hard for the sated and the mighty to grasp the meaning of God's judgement and God's mercy. And for one who has been disappointed in mistaken belief, and who has become inwardly undisciplined, it is hard to attain to the simplicity of the surrender of the heart to Jesus Christ. That is not said in order either to excuse or to discourage those whom these things have befallen. They must know, on the contrary, that it is precisely to the depths of downfall, of guilt and of misery, that God stoops down in Jesus Christ; that precisely the dispossessed, the humiliated and the exploited, are especially near to the justice and mercy of God; that it is to the undisciplined that Jesus Christ offers His help and His strength; and that the truth is ready to set upon firm ground those who stray and despair.

The New Life

JESUS CHRIST WHO ROSE AGAIN—this means that God out of His love and omnipotence sets an end to death and calls a new creation into life, imparts new life. 'Old things are passed away' (II Cor. 5:17). 'Behold, I make all things new' (Rev. 21:5). Already in the midst of the old world, resurrection has dawned, as a last sign of its end and of its future, and at the same time as a living reality. Jesus rose again as a man, and by so doing He gave men the gift of the resurrection. Thus man remains man, even though he is a new, a risen man, who in no way resembles the old man. Until he crosses the frontier of his death, even though he has already risen again with Christ, he remains in the world of penultimate, the world into which Jesus entered and the world in which the cross stands. Thus, so long as the earth continues, even the resurrection does not annul the penultimate, but the eternal life, the new life, breaks in with ever greater power into the earthly life and wins its space for itself within it.

We have tried to make clear the unity and the diversity of the incarnation, the cross and the resurrection. Christian life is life with the incarnate, crucified and risen Christ, whose word confronts us in its entirety in the message of the justification of the sinner by grace alone. Christian life means being a man through the efficacy of the incarnation; it means being sentenced and pardoned through the efficacy of the cross; and it means living a new life through the efficacy of the resurrection. There cannot be one of these without the rest.

The Past

O HAPPINESS BELOVED, and pain beloved in heaviness,
you went from me.
What shall I call you? Anguish, life, blessedness,
part of myself, my heart—the past?
The door was slammed;
I hear your steps depart and slowly die away.
What now remains for me—torment, delight, desire?
This only do I know: that with you, all has gone.
But do you feel how I now grasp at you
and so clutch hold of you
that it must hurt you?
How I so rend you
that your blood gushes out,
simply to be sure that you are near me,
a life in earthly form, complete?
Do you divine my terrible desire
for my own suffering,
my eager wish to see my own blood flow,
only that all may not go under,
lost in the past?

Life, what have you done to me?
Why did you come? Why did you go?
Past, when you flee from me,
are you not still my past, my own?
As o'er the sea the sun sinks ever faster,
as if it moved towards the darkness,
so does your image sink and sink and sink
without a pause

into the ocean of the past,
and waves engulf it.
As the warm breath dissolves
in the cool morning air,
so does your image vanish from me,
and I forget your face, your hands, your form.
There comes a smile, a glance, a greeting;
it fades, dissolves,
comfortless, distant,
is destroyed, is past.

I would inhale the fragrance of your being,
absorb it, stay with it,
as on hot summer days the heavy blossoms
    welcoming the bees
intoxicate them,
as privet makes the hawk-moths drunken—
but a harsh gust destroys both scent and blossoms,
and I stand like a fool
seeking a past that vanished.
It is as if parts of my flesh were torn out with red-hot
    pincers,
when you, a part of my life that is past, so quickly
    depart.
Raging defiance and anger beset me,
reckless and profitless questions I fling into space.
'Why, why, why?' I keep on repeating—
why cannot my senses hold you,
life now passing, now past?
Thus I will think, and think anew,
until I find what I have lost.

But I feel
that everything around me, over, under me
is smiling at me, unmoved, enigmatic,
smiling at my hopeless efforts

to grasp the wind,
to capture what has gone.

Evil comes into my eye and soul;
what I see, I hate;
I hate what moves me;
all that lives I hate, all that is lovely,
all that would recompense me for my loss.
I want my life; I claim my own life back again,
my past, yourself.
Yourself. A tear wells up and fills my eye;
can I, in mists of tears,
regain your image,
yourself entire?
But I will not weep;
only the strong are helped by tears,
weaklings they make ill.

Wearily I come to the evening;
welcome are bed and oblivion
now that my own is denied me.
Night, blot out what separates, give me oblivion,
in charity perform your kindly office;
to you I trust myself.
But night is wise and mighty,
wiser than I, and mightier than day,
What no earthly power can do,
what is denied to thoughts and senses, to defiance, to
    tears,
night brings me, in its bounty overflowing.
Unharmed by hostile time,
pure, free, and whole,
you are brought to me by dream,
you, my past, my life,
Close to you I waken in the dead of night,
and start with fear—

are you lost to me once more? Is it always vainly that I
    seek you,
you, my past?
I stretch my hands out,
and I pray—
and a new thing now I hear:
'The past will come to you once more,
and be your life's enduring part,
through thanks and repentance.
Feel in the past God's forgiveness and goodness,
pray him to keep you today and tomorrow.'

Justification

...NOT FOR A MOMENT can faith and evil intention exist side
by side. When a man undergoes justification he is given
everything, but only faith brings justification. When a
man encounters Christ, everything that Christ is and has
is made the property of this man; yet my life is justified
solely by that which is the property of Christ and never by
that which has become my own property. Thus the
heaven opens over man's head and the joyful tidings of
God's salvation in Jesus Christ come down like a shout of
rejoicing from heaven to earth, and man believes, and, in
believing, he has already received Christ to himself; he
possesses everything. He lives before God.

He never knew before what life is. He did not understand
himself. Only by his own potentialities or by his own
achievement could he try to understand himself and to
justify his life. In this way he could justify himself to
himself and to a god of his own imagining, but he could
have no means of access to the potentialities and the works

of the living God; he could have no conception of a life which should proceed from these potentialities and works of the living God. He could not conceive of a life on a foundation other than himself, sustained by a power other than his own. Yet this is the life that he found when Christ justified him in His way. He lost his own life to Christ, and Christ became his life. 'I live; yet not I, but Christ liveth in me' (Gal. 2:20). Christian life is the life of Christ.

Conformation

TO BE CONFORMED with the Risen One—that is to be a new man before God. In the midst of death he is in life. In the midst of sin he is righteous. In the midst of the old he is new. His secret remains hidden from the world. He lives because Christ lives, and lives in Christ alone. 'Christ is my life' (Phil 1:21). So long as the glory of Christ is hidden, so long, too, does the glory of his new life remain 'hidden with Christ in God' (Col. 3:3). But he who knows espies already here and there a gleam of what is to come. The new man lives in the world like any other man. Often there is little to distinguish him from the rest. Nor does he attach importance to distinguishing himself, but only to distinguishing Christ for the sake of his brethren. Transfigured though he is in the form of the Risen One, here he bears only the sign of the cross and the judgement. By bearing it willingly he shows himself to be the one who has received the Holy Spirit and who is united with Jesus Christ in incomparable love and fellowship.

The form of Jesus Christ takes form in man. Man does not take on an independent form of his own, but what gives him form and what maintains him in the new form is always solely the form of Jesus Christ Himself. It is therefore not a vain imitation or repetition of Christ's form but Christ's form itself which takes form in man. And again, man is not transformed into a form which is alien to him, the form of God, but into his own form, the form which is essentially proper to him. Man becomes man because God became man. But man does not become God. It is not he, therefore, who was or is able to accomplish his own transformation, but it is God who changes his form into the form of man, so that man may become, not indeed God, but, in the eyes of God, man.

In Christ there was re-created the form of man before God. It was not an outcome of the place or the time, of the climate or the race, of the individual or the society, or of religion or of taste, but quite simply of the life of mankind as such, that mankind at this point recognized its image and its hope. What befell Christ had befallen mankind. It is a mystery, for which there is no explanation, that only a part of mankind recognize the form of their Redeemer. The longing of the Incarnate to take form in all men is as yet still unsatisfied. He bore the form of man as a whole, and yet He can take form only in a small band. These are His Church.

Christ and His Body

THROUGH HIS SPIRIT, the crucified and risen Lord exists as the Church, as the new man. It is just as true to say that his Body is the new humanity as to say that he is God incarnate dwelling in eternity. As the fulness of the Godhead dwells in Christ bodily, so the Christian believers are filled with Christ (Col. 2:9; Eph. 3:19). Indeed, they are themselves that fulness in so far as they are in the Body and in so far as it is he alone who filleth all in all.

When we have recognized the unity between Christ and his Body, the Church, we must also hold fast to the complementary truth of Christ's Lordship over the Body. That is why St Paul, as he comes to develop the theme of the Body of Christ, calls him the Head of the Body (Eph. 1.22; Col. 1:18; 2:19). This assertion symbolizes and preserves the truth that Christ stands over against his Church. The historical fact in the story of our redemption which makes this truth essential, and rules out any idea of a mystical fusion between Christ and his Church, is the Ascension of Christ (and his Second Coming). The same Christ who is present in his Church will also come again. It is the same Lord and the same Church in both places, and it is one and the same Body, whether we think of his presence on earth or of his coming again on the clouds of heaven. But it makes a great deal of difference whether we are here or there. So it is necessary to give due weight both to the unity of Christ and his Church and to their distinction.

The Church is one man; it is the Body of Christ. But it is also many, a fellowship of members (Rom. 12:5; I Cor. 12:12 ff).

The Church

IF GOD IN JESUS CHRIST claims space in the world, even though it be only a stable 'because there was no room in the inn' (Luke 2:7), then in this narrow space He comprises together the whole reality of the world at once and reveals the ultimate basis of this reality. And so, too, the Church of Jesus Christ is the place, in other words the space in the world, at which the reign of Jesus Christ over the whole world is evidenced and proclaimed. This space of the Church, then, is not something which exists on its own account. It is from the outset something which reaches out far beyond itself, for indeed it is not the space of some kind of cultural association such as would have to fight for its own survival in the world, but it is the place where testimony is given to the foundation of all reality in Jesus Christ. The Church is the place where testimony and serious thought are given to God's reconciliation of the world with Himself in Christ, to His having so loved the world that He gave His Son for its sake. The space of the Church is not there in order to try to deprive the world of a piece of its territory, but precisely in order to prove to the world that it is still the world, the world which is loved by God and reconciled with Him. The Church has neither the wish nor the obligation to extend her space to cover the space of the world. She asks for no more space than she needs for the purpose of serving the world by bearing witness to Jesus Christ and to the reconciliation of the world with God through Him. The only way in which the Church can defend her own territory is by fighting not for it but for the salvation of the world. Otherwise the Church becomes a 'religious society' which fights in its own interest and thereby ceases at once to be the Church of God and of the world. And so the first demand which is made of those who belong to God's Church is not that they should be something in themselves, not that they should, for example, set up some religious organization or that they should lead lives of piety, but that they shall be witnesses to Jesus Christ before the world. It is for this task that the Holy Spirit equips those to whom He gives Himself. It is, of course, to be assumed that this testimony before the world can be delivered in the right way only if it springs from a hallowed life in the congregation of God. But a genuine hallowed life in the congregation of God differs from any pious imitation of it in that it at the same time impels a man to testify before the world.

Christ the Center

CHRIST IS *the* new creature. Thereby he shows all other creatures to be old creatures. Nature stands under the curse which God laid upon Adam's ground. It was the originally created Word of God, proclaiming it freely. As the fallen creation it is now dumb, enslaved under the guilt of man. Like history, it suffers from the loss of its meaning and its freedom. It waits expectantly for a new freedom. Nature, unlike man and history, will not be reconciled, but it will be set free for a new freedom. Its catastrophes are the dull will to set itself free, to show its power over man and by its own right to be a new creature, which it has made anew itself.

In the sacrament of the Church, the old enslaved creature is set free to its new freedom. As the centre of human existence and of history, Christ was the fulfilment of the unfulfilled law, i.e. their reconciliation. But nature is creation under the curse—not guilt, for it lacks freedom. Thus nature finds in Christ as its centre, not reconciliation, but redemption. Once again, this redemption, which happens in Christ, is not evident, nor can it be proved, but it is proclaimed. The word of preaching is that enslaved nature is redeemed in hope. A sign of this is given in the sacraments, where elements of the old creation are become elements of the new. In the sacraments they are set free from their dumbness and proclaim directly to the believer the new creative Word of God. They no longer need the explanation of man. Enslaved nature does not speak the Word of God to us directly. But the sacraments do. In the sacrament, Christ is the mediator between nature and God and stands for all creation before God.

To sum up, we must continue to emphasize that Christ is truly the centre of human existence, the centre of history and now also the centre of nature. But these three aspects can only be distinguished from each other *in abstracto*. In fact, human existence is also and always history, always and also nature. The mediator as fulfiller of the law and liberator of creation is all this for the whole of human existence. He is the same who is intercessor and *pro me*, and who is himself the end of the old world and the beginning of the new world of God.

The Preacher

WHAT THE CHURCH PROCLAIMS is the word of the revelation of God in Jesus Christ. This word does not proceed from any man's own heart or understanding or character; it comes down to man from heaven, from the will and the mercy of God; it is a word commanded and instituted by Jesus Christ, and from this it follows that the word, by the manner of its coming, establishes a clearly differentiated relation of superiority and inferiority. Above there is the office of proclamation, and below there is the listening congregation. In the place of God and of Jesus Christ there stands before the congregation the bearer of the office of preaching with his proclamation. The preacher is not the spokesman of the congregation, but, if the expression may be allowed, he is the spokesman of God before the congregation. He is authorized to teach, to admonish and to comfort, to forgive sin, but also to retain sin. And at the same time he is the shepherd, the pastor of the flock. This office is instituted directly by Jesus Christ Himself; it does not derive its legitimation from the will of the congregation but from the will of Jesus Christ. It is established *in* the congregation and not *by* the congregation, and at the same time it is *with* the congregation. When this office is exercised in the congregation to its full extent, life is infused into all the other offices of the congregation, which can after all only be subservient to the office of the divine word; for wherever the word of God rules alone, there will be found faith and service. The congregation which is being awakened by the proclamation of the word of God will demonstrate the genuineness of its faith by honouring the office of preaching in its unique glory and by serving it with all its powers; it will not rely on its own faith or on the universal priesthood of all believers in order to depreciate the office of preaching, to place obstacles in its way, or even to try to make it subordinate to itself. The superior status of the office of preaching is preserved from abuse, and against danger from without, precisely by a genuine subordination of the congregation, that is to say, by faith, prayer and service, but not by a suppression or disruption of the divine order or by a perverse desire for superiority on the part of the congregation.

The Saints

THE ECCLESIA *Christi*, the disciple community, has been torn from the clutches of the world. Of course it still has to live in the world, but it is made into one body, with its own sphere of sovereignty, and its own claim to living-space. It is the holy Church (Eph. 5:27), the community of the saints (I Cor. 14:33), and its members are called to be saints (Rom. 1:7), sanctified in Jesus Christ (I Cor. 1:2), chosen and set apart before the foundation of the world (Eph. 1:4). The object of their calling in Jesus Christ, and of their election before the foundation of the world, was that they should be holy and without blemish (Eph. 1:4). Christ had surrendered his body to death that he might present his own holy and without blemish and unreproveable before him (Col. 1:22). The fruit of their liberation from sin through the death of Christ is that whereas they once surrendered their members' servants to iniquity, they may now use them in the service of righteousness unto sanctification (Rom. 6:19–22).

The Task of the Church

WHAT THE WEST is doing is to refuse to accept its historical inheritance for what it is. The west is becoming hostile towards Christ. This is the peculiar situation of our time, and it is genuine decay. Amid the disruption of the whole established order of things there stand the Christian Churches as guardians of the heritage of the Middle Ages and of the Reformation and especially as witnesses of the miracle of God in Jesus Christ 'yesterday, and today, and for ever' (He. 13:8). And at their side there stands the 'restrainer', that is to say the remaining force of order which still opposes effective resistance to the process of decay. The task of the Church is without parallel. The *corpus christianum* is broken asunder. The *corpus Christi* confronts a hostile world. The world has known Christ and has turned its back on Him, and it is to this world that the Church must now prove that Christ is the living Lord.

Even while she waits for the last day, the Church, as the bearer of a historical inheritance, is bound by an obligation to the historical future. Her vision of the end of all things must not hinder her in the fulfilment of her historical responsibility. She must leave not only the end to God's decision, but also the possibility of the continuance of history. She must set her mind on both. In devoting herself to her proper task, that is to say to preaching the risen Jesus Christ, the Church strikes a mortal blow at the spirit of destruction. The 'restrainer', the force of order, sees in the Church an ally, and, whatever other elements of order may remain, will seek a place at her side. Justice, truth, science, art, culture, humanity, liberty, patriotism, all at last, after long straying from the path, are once more finding their way back to their fountain-head. The more central the message of the Church, the greater now will be her effectiveness. Her suffering presents an infinitely greater danger to the spirit of destruction than does any political power which may still remain. But through her message of the living Lord Jesus Christ the Church makes it clear that she is not concerned merely for the mainte-nance and preservation of the past. Even the forces of order she compels to listen and to turn back. Yet she does not reject those who come to her and seek to place themselves at her side. She leaves it to God's governance of the world to decide whether He will permit the success of the forces of order and whether she, the Church, while still preserving the essential distinction between herself and these forces, even though she unreservedly allies herself with them, will be allowed to pass on to the future that historical inheritance which bears within it the bless-ing and the guilt of past generations.

The Battlefield

BECAUSE IT IS SANCTIFIED by the seal of the Spirit, the Church is always in the battlefield, waging a war to prevent the breaking of the seal, whether from within or from without, and struggling to prevent the world from becoming the Church and the Church from becoming the world. The sanctification of the Church is really a defensive war, for the place which has been given to the Body of Christ on earth. The separation of the Church and the world from one another is the crusade which the Church fights for the sanctuary of God on earth.

This sanctuary can only exist in the visible Church. But—and here we come to the second point—the very fact that it is separated from the world means that while the Church lives in the sanctuary of God something of the world still lives in the Church. That is why it is the duty of the saints to walk worthily of their calling and of the gospel in every sphere of life (Eph. 4:1; Phil. 1:27; Col. 1:10; I Thess. 2:12). But the only way to do this is by daily recalling the gospel on which their whole life depends. "Ye were washed, ye were sanctified, ye were justified" (I Cor. 6:11). It is by living daily on this recollection that the saints are sanctified. And the gospel of which they are to be worthy is that which proclaims the death of the world and the flesh, and their own crucifixion and death with Christ on the cross and through baptism, which proclaims that sin can no longer have dominion over them because its sovereignty has already been broken, and that it is no longer possible for the Christian to sin. "Whosoever is begotten of God doeth no sin" (I John 3:9).

Confession of Guilt

...EVEN THE MOST SECRET SIN of the individual is defilement and destruction of the body of Christ (I Cor. 6:15). From the desires that are in our bodily members come murder and envy, strife and war (Jas. 4:1ff.). If my share in this is so small as to seem negligible, that still cannot set my mind at rest; for now it is not a matter of apportioning the blame, but I must acknowledge that precisely my sin is to blame for all. I am guilty of uncontrolled desire. I am guilty of cowardly silence at a time when I ought to have spoken. I am guilty of hypocrisy and untruthfulness in the face of force. I have been lacking in compassion and I have denied the poorest of my brethren. I am guilty of disloyalty and of apostasy from Christ. What does it matter to you whether others are guilty too? I can excuse any sin of another, but my own sin alone remains guilt which I can never excuse. It is not a morbidly egotistical distortion of reality, but it is the essential character of a genuine confession of guilt that it is incapable of apportioning blame and pleading a case, but is rather the acknowledgement of one's own sin of Adam. And it is senseless to try to oppose this acknowledgement with an argument *ad absurdum* by pointing out that there are innumerable individuals each of whom must in this way be conscious of being to blame for the whole. For indeed these innumerable individuals are united in the collective personality of the Church. It is in them and through them that the Church confesses and acknowledges her guilt.

Costly Grace

CHEAP GRACE is the deadly enemy of our Church. We are fighting to-day for costly grace.

Cheap grace means grace sold on the market like cheapjacks' wares. The sacraments, the forgiveness of sin, and the consolations of religion are thrown away at cut prices. Grace is presented as the Church's inexhaustible treasury, from which she showers blessings with generous hands, without asking questions or fixing limits. Grace without price; grace without cost! The essence of grace, we suppose, is that the account has been paid in advance; and, because it has been paid, everything can be had for nothing. Since the cost was infinite, the possibilities of using and spending it are infinite. What would grace be if it were not cheap?

Cheap grace means grace as a doctrine, a principle, a system. It means forgiveness of sins proclaimed as a general truth, the love of God taught as the Christian "conception" of God. An intellectual assent to that idea is held to be of itself sufficient to secure remission of sins. The Church which holds the correct doctrine of grace has, it is supposed, *ipso facto* a part in that grace. In such a Church the world finds a cheap covering for its sins; no contrition is required, still less any real desire to be delivered from sin. Cheap grace therefore amounts to a denial of the living Word of God, in fact, a denial of the Incarnation of the Word of God.

. . . Cheap grace is the preaching of forgiveness without requiring repentance, baptism without Church discipline, Communion without confession, absolution without per-

sonal confession. Cheap grace is grace without discipleship, grace without the cross, grace without Jesus Christ,
living and incarnate.

Costly grace is the treasure hidden in the field; for the
sake of it a man will gladly go and sell all that he has. It is
the pearl of great price to buy which the merchant will sell
all his goods. It is the kingly rule of Christ, for whose sake
a man will pluck out the eye which causes him to stumble,
it is the call of Jesus Christ at which the disciple leaves his
nets and follows him.

Costly grace is the gospel which must be *sought* again
and again, the gift which must be *asked* for, the door at
which a man must *knock*.

Such grace is *costly* because it calls us to follow, and it is
grace because it calls us to follow *Jesus Christ*. It is costly
because it costs a man his life, and it is grace because it
gives a man the only true life. It is costly because it
condemns sin, and grace because it justifies the sinner.
Above all, it is *costly* because it cost God the life of his Son:
"ye were bought at a price," and what has cost God much
cannot be cheap for us. Above all, it is *grace* because God
did not reckon his Son too dear a price to pay for our life,
but delivered him up for us. Costly grace is the Incarnation of God.

Costly grace is the sanctuary of God; it has to be
protected from the world, and not thrown to the dogs. It is
therefore the living word, the Word of God, which he
speaks as it pleases him. Costly grace confronts us as a
gracious call to follow Jesus, it comes as a word of
forgiveness to the broken spirit and the contrite heart.
Grace is costly because it compels a man to submit to the
yoke of Christ and follow him; it is grace because Jesus
says: "My yoke is easy and my burden is light."

The New Fellowship

THE MEMBER of the Body of Christ has been delivered from the world and called out of it. He must give the world a visible proof of his calling, not only by sharing in the Church's worship and discipline, but also through the new fellowship of brotherly living. If the world despises one of the brethren, the Christian will love and serve him. If the world does him violence, the Christian will succour and comfort him. If the world dishonours and insults him, the Christian will sacrifice his own honour to cover his brother's shame. Where the world seeks gain, the Christian will renounce it. Where the world exploits, he will dispossess himself, and where the world oppresses, he will stoop down and raise up the oppressed. If the world refuses justice, the Christian will pursue mercy, and if the world takes refuge in lies, he will open his mouth for the dumb, and bear testimony to the truth. For the sake of the brother, be he Jew or Greek, bond or free, strong or weak, noble or base, he will renounce all fellowship with the world. For the Christian serves the fellowship of the Body of Christ, and he cannot hide it from the world. He is called out of the world to follow Christ.

The Followers of Christ

THE CHURCH of Jesus cannot arbitrarily break off all contact with those who refuse his call. It is called to follow the Lord by promise and commandment. That must suffice. All judgement of others and separation from them must be left to him who chose the Church according to his good purpose, and not for any merit or achievement of its own. The separation of Church and world is not effected by the Church itself, but by the word of its calling.

A little band of men, the followers of Christ, are separated from the rest of the world. The disciples are few in number, and will always be few. This saying of Jesus forestalls all exaggerated hopes of success. Never let a disciple of Jesus pin his hopes on large numbers. "Few there be...." The rest of the world are many, and will always be many. But they are on the road to perdition. The only comfort the disciples have in face of this prospect is the promise of life and eternal fellowship with Jesus.

The path of discipleship is narrow, and it is fatally easy to miss one's way and stray from the path, even after years of discipleship. And it is hard to find. On either side of the narrow path deep chasms yawn. To be called to a life of extraordinary quality, to live up to it, and yet to be unconscious of it is indeed a narrow way. To confess and testify to the truth as it is in Jesus, and at the same time to love the enemies of that truth, his enemies and ours, and to love them with the infinite love of Jesus Christ, is indeed a narrow way. To believe the promise of Jesus that his followers shall possess the earth, and at the same time to face our enemies unarmed and defenceless, preferring to incur injustice rather than to do wrong ourselves, is indeed a narrow way. To see the weakness and wrong in others, and at the same time refrain from judging them; to deliver the gospel message without casting pearls before swine, is indeed a narrow way. The way is unutterably hard, and at every moment we are in danger of straying from it. If we regard this way as one we follow in obedience to an external command, if we are afraid of ourselves all the time, it is indeed an impossible way. But if we behold Jesus Christ going on before step by step, we shall not go astray. But if we worry about the dangers that beset us, if we gaze at the road instead of at him who goes before, we are already straying from the path. For he is himself the way, the narrow way and the strait gate. He, and he alone, is our journey's end. When we know that, we are able to proceed along the narrow way through the strait gate of the cross, and on to eternal life, and the very narrowness of the road will increase our certainty. The way which the Son of God trod on earth, and the way which we too must tread as citizens of two worlds on the razor edge between this world and the kingdom of heaven, could hardly be a broad way. The narrow way is bound to be right.

Pray for Forgiveness

...WHEREVER IT BECOMES VISIBLE on a large scale, wherever the world looks at the Christians and feels obliged to say, as it said in the earliest days, "See how these Christians love one another," the saints must then take special care to keep their eyes on him alone, to ignore any good they may have achieved themselves, and to pray fervently for forgiveness. The same Christians who have claimed the privilege of being no longer under the dominion of sin, will confess: "If we say we have no sin, we deceive ourselves, and the truth is not in us. If we confess our sins, he is faithful and just to forgive us our sins, and to cleanse us from all unrighteousness. If we say that we have not sinned, we make him a liar, and his word is not in us. My little children these things I write unto you, that ye may not sin. And if any man sin, we have an advocate with the Father, Jesus Christ the righteous" (I John 1:8–2:1). This is exactly how the Lord himself taught us to pray—"Forgive us our trespasses." He charged us never to tire of forgiving one another (Eph. 4:32; Matt. 18:21ff). Brotherly forgiveness makes room for the forgiveness of Jesus to enter into their common life. Instead of seeing their neighbours as men who have injured them, they see them as men for whom Christ has won forgiveness on the cross. They meet on the basis of their common sanctification through the cross of Christ.

Good Works

THROUGH GOD'S OWN ACTION in Christ we have been saved and not through our own works. We can never boast about them, for we are ourselves his workmanship. Yet it remains true that the whole purpose of our new creation in Christ is that in him we might attain unto good works.

But all our good works are the works of God himself, the works for which he has prepared us beforehand. Good works then are ordained for the sake of salvation, but they are in the end those which God himself works within us. They are his gift, but it is *our* task to walk in them at every moment of our lives, knowing all the time that any good works of our own could never help us to abide before the judgement of God. We cling in faith to Christ and his works alone. For we have the promise that those who are in Christ Jesus will be enabled to do good works, which will testify for them in the day of judgement. They will be preserved and sanctified until the last day. All we can do is believe in God's Word, rely on his promise, and walk in the good works which he has prepared for us.

From this it follows that we can never be conscious of our good works. Our sanctification is veiled from our eyes until the last day, when all secrets will be disclosed. If we want to see some results here and assess our own spiritual state, and have not the patience to wait, we have our reward. The moment we begin to feel satisfied that we are making some progress along the road of sanctification, it is all the more necessary to repent and confess that all our righteousnesses are as filthy rags. Yet the Christian life is not one of gloom, but of ever increasing joy in the Lord. God alone knows our good works, all we know is his good work. We can do no more than hearken to his commandment, carry on and rely on his grace, walk in his commandments, and—sin. All the time our new righteousness, our sanctification, the light which is meant to shine, are veiled from our eyes. The left hand knows not what the right hand does. But we believe, and are well assured, "that he which began a good work in you will perfect it until the day of Jesus Christ" (Phil. 1:6). In that day Christ will show us the good works of which we were unaware. While we knew it not, we gave him food, drink and clothing and visited him, and while we knew it not we rejected him. Great will be our astonishment in that day, and we shall then realize that it is not our works which remain but the work which God has wrought through us in his good time without any effort of will and intention on our part (Matt. 25:31ff). Once again we simply are to look away from ourselves to him who has himself accomplished all things for us and to follow him.

Through and in Jesus Christ

CHRISTIANITY MEANS COMMUNITY through Jesus Christ and in Jesus Christ. No Christian community is more or less than this. Whether it be a brief, single encounter or the daily fellowship of years, Christian community is only this. We belong to one another only through and in Jesus Christ.

What does this mean? It means, first, that a Christian needs others because of Jesus Christ. It means, second, that a Christian comes to others only through Jesus Christ. It means, third, that in Jesus Christ we have been chosen from eternity, accepted in time, and united for eternity.

Christ Among Us

...IT IS THE MYSTERY of the community that Christ is in her and, only through her, reaches to men. Christ exists among us as community, as Church in the hiddenness of history. The Church is the hidden Christ among us. Now therefore man is never alone, but he exists only through the community which brings him Christ, which incorporates him in itself, takes him into its life. Man in Christ is man in community; where he exists is community. But because at the same time as individual he is fully a member of the community, therefore here alone is the continuity of his existence preserved in Christ. Therefore man can no longer understand himself from himself, but only from Christ. . . .

The Day's Beginning

"LET THE WORD OF CHRIST dwell in you richly" (Col. 3:16). The Old Testament day begins at evening and ends with the going down of the sun. It is the time of expectation. The day of the New Testament church begins with the break of day and ends with the dawning light of the next morning. It is the time of fulfilment, the resurrection of the Lord. At night Christ was born, a light in darkness; noonday turned to night when Christ suffered and died on the Cross. But in the dawn of Easter morning Christ rose in victory from the grave.

> Ere yet the dawn hath filled the skies
> Behold my Saviour Christ arise,
> He chaseth from us sin and night,
> And brings us joy and life and light.
> Hallelujah

So sang the church of the Reformation. Christ is the "Sun of righteousness," risen upon the expectant congregation (Mal. 4:2), and they that love him shall "be as the sun when he goeth forth in his might" (Judges 5:31). The early morning belongs to the Church of the risen Christ. At the break of light it remembers the morning on which death and sin lay prostrate in defeat and new life and salvation were given to mankind.

Morning Prayers

O God, early in the morning I cry to you.
Help me to pray
And to concentrate my thoughts on you;
I cannot do this alone.

In me there is darkness,
But with you there is light;
I am lonely, but you do not leave me;
I am feeble in heart, but with you there is help;
I am restless, but with you there is peace.
In me there is bitterness, but with you there is patience;
I do not understand your ways,
But you know the way for me.

O heavenly Father,
I praise and thank you
For the peace of the night;
I praise and thank you for this new day;
I praise and thank you for all your goodness
and faithfulness throughout my life.

You have granted me many blessings;
Now let me also accept what is hard
from your hand.
You will lay on me no more
than I can bear.

Editor's note: Written for fellow prisoners Christmas 1943.

You make all things work together for good
for your children.

Lord Jesus Christ,
You were poor
and in distress, a captive and forsaken as I am.
You know all man's troubles;
You abide with me
when all men fail me;
You remember and seek me;
It is your will that I should know you
and turn to you.
Lord, I hear your call and follow;
Help me.

O Holy Spirit,
Give me faith that will protect me
from despair, from passions, and from vice;
Give me such love for God and men
as will blot out all hatred and bitterness;
Give me the hope that will deliver me
from fear and faint-heartedness.

O holy and merciful God,
my Creator and Redeemer,
my Judge and Saviour,
You know me and all that I do.
You hate and punish evil without respect of persons
in this world and the next;
You forgive the sins of those
who sincerely pray for forgiveness;
You love goodness, and reward it on this earth
with a clear conscience,

and, in the world to come,
with a crown of righteousness.

I remember in your presence all my loved ones,
my fellow-prisoners, and all who in this house
perform their hard service;
Lord, have mercy.

Restore me to liberty,
and enable me so to live now
that I may answer before you and before men.
Lord, whatever this day may bring,
Your name be praised.
Amen.

Evening Prayers

O Lord my God, thank you
for bringing this day to a close;
Thank you for giving me rest
in body and soul.
Your hand has been over me
and has guarded and preserved me.
Forgive my lack of faith
and any wrong that I have done today,
and help me to forgive all who have wronged me.

Let me sleep in peace under your protection,
and keep me from all the temptations of darkness.

Into your hands I commend my loved ones
and all who dwell in this house;
I commend to you my body and soul.
O God, your holy name be praised.
Amen.

The Hiddenness of Prayer

TRUE PRAYER is done in secret, but this does not rule out the fellowship of prayer altogether, however clearly we may be aware of its dangers. In the last resort it is immaterial whether we pray in the open street or in the secrecy of our chambers, whether briefly or lengthily, in the Litany of the Church, or with the sigh of one who knows not what he should pray for. True prayer does not depend either on the individual or the whole body of the faithful, but solely upon the knowledge that our heavenly Father knows our needs. That makes God the sole object of our prayers, and frees us from a false confidence in our own prayerful efforts.

> After this manner therefore pray ye: Our Father which art in heaven, Hallowed be thy name. Thy kingdom come. Thy will be done, as in heaven, so on earth. Give us this day our daily bread. And forgive us our debts, as we also have forgiven our debtors. And bring us not into temptation, but deliver us from the evil one. For if ye forgive not men their trespasses, neither will your Father forgive your trespasses. (Matt. 6:9–15)

Jesus told his disciples not only *how* to pray, but also *what* to pray. The Lord's Prayer is not merely the pattern prayer, it is the way Christians *must* pray. If they pray this prayer, God will certainly hear them. The Lord's Prayer is the quintessence of prayer. A disciple's prayer is founded on and circumscribed by it. Once again Jesus does not leave his disciples in ignorance; he teaches them the

Lord's Prayer and so leads them to a clear understanding of prayer.

Baptism

BAPTISM IS NOT AN OFFER made by man to God, but an offer made by Christ to man. It is grounded solely on the will of Jesus Christ, as expressed in his gracious call. Baptism is essentially passive—*being baptized, suffering* the call of Christ. In baptism man becomes Christ's own possession. When the name of Christ is spoken over the candidate, he becomes a partaker in this Name, and is baptized "*into* Jesus Christ" (εἰς, Rom. 6:3; Gal. 3:27; Matt. 28:19). From that moment he belongs to Jesus Christ. He is wrested from the dominion of the world, and passes into the ownership of Christ.

Baptism therefore betokens a *breach*. Christ invades the realm of Satan, lays hands on his own, and creates for himself his Church. By this act past and present are rent asunder. The old order is passed away, and all things have become new. This breach is not effected by man's tearing off his own chains through some unquenchable longing for a new life of freedom. The breach has been effected by Christ long since, and in baptism it is effected in our own lives. We are now deprived of our direct relationship with all God-given realities of life. Christ the Mediator has stepped in between us and them. The baptized Christian has ceased to belong to the world and is no longer its slave. He belongs to Christ alone, and his relationship with the world is mediated through him.

The breach with the world is complete. It demands and

produces the death of the old man.[1] In baptism a man dies together with his old world. This death, no less than baptism itself, is a passive event. It is not as though a man must achieve his own death through various kinds of renunciation and mortification. That would never be the death of the old man which Christ demands. The old man cannot will his own death or kill himself. He can only die in, through and with Christ. Christ is his death. For the sake of fellowship with Christ, and in that fellowship alone a man dies. In fellowship with Christ and through the grace of baptism he receives his death as a gift.[2] This death is a gift of grace: a man can never accomplish it by himself. The old man and his sin are judged and condemned, but out of this judgement a new man arises, who has died to the world and to sin.

[1] Even Jesus himself referred to his death as a baptism, and promised that his disciples would share this baptism of death (Mark 10:39; Luke 12:50).
[2] Schlatter also takes I Cor. 15:29 as a reference to the baptism of martyrdom.

The Gift of Baptism

IT IS THEIR BAPTISM into the Body of Christ which assures all Christians of their full share in the life of Christ and the Church. It is wrong, and contrary to the New Testament, to limit the gift of baptism to participation in the sermon and the Lord's Supper, i.e. to participation in the means of grace, or to the right to hold office or perform a ministry in the Church. On the contrary, baptism confers the privilege of participation in all the activities of the Body of Christ in every department of life. To allow a baptized brother to take part in the worship of the Church, but to refuse to have anything to do with him in everyday life, is to subject him to abuse and contempt. If we do that, we are guilty of the very Body of Christ. And if we grant the baptized brother the right to the gifts of salvation, but refuse him the gifts necessary to earthly life or knowingly leave him in material need and distress, we are holding up the gifts of salvation to ridicule and behaving as liars. If the Holy Ghost has spoken and we listen instead to the call of blood and nature, or to our personal sympathies or antipathies, we are profaning the sacrament. When a man is baptized into the Body of Christ not only is his personal status as regards salvation changed, but also the relationship of daily life.

From 'Thoughts on the Day of Baptism of Dietrich Wilhelm Rüdinger Bethge' May 1944

TODAY YOU WILL BE BAPTIZED A CHRISTIAN. All those great ancient words of the Christian proclamation will be spoken over you, and the command of Jesus Christ to baptize will be carried out on you, without your knowing anything about it. But we are once again being driven right back to the beginnings of our understanding. Reconciliation and redemption, regeneration and the Holy Spirit, love of our enemies, cross and resurrection, life in Christ and Christian discipleship—all these things are so difficult and so remote that we hardly venture any more to speak of them. In the traditional words and acts we suspect that there may be something quite new and revolutionary, though we cannot as yet grasp or express it. That is our own fault. Our church, which has been fighting in these years only for its self-preservation, as though that were an end in itself, is incapable of taking the word of reconciliation and redemption to mankind and the world. Our earlier words are therefore bound to lose their force and cease, and our being Christians today will be limited to two things: prayer and righteous action among men. All Christian thinking, speaking, and organizing must be born anew out of this prayer and action. By the time you have grown up, the church's form will have changed greatly. We are not yet out of the melting-pot, and any attempt to help the church prematurely to a new expansion of its organization will merely delay its conversion and purification. It is not for us to prophesy the day (though the day will come) when men will once more be called so to utter the word of God that the world will be changed and renewed by it. It will be a new language, perhaps quite non-religious, but liberating and redeeming—as was Jesus' language; it will shock people and yet overcome them by its power; it will be the language of a new righteousness and truth, proclaiming God's peace with men and the coming of his kingdom. 'They shall fear and tremble because of all the good and all the prosperity I provide for it' (Jer. 33:9). Till then the Christian cause will be a silent and hidden affair, but there will be those who pray and do right and wait for God's own time. May you be one of them, and may it be said of you one day, 'The path of the righteous is like the light of dawn, which shines brighter and brighter till full day' (Prov. 4:18).

Vocation

IN THE ENCOUNTER with Jesus Christ man hears the call of God and in it the calling to life in the fellowship of Jesus Christ. Divine grace comes upon man and lays claim to him. It is not man who seeks out grace in its own place— God dwelleth in the light which no man can approach unto (I Tim. 6:16), but it is grace which seeks and finds man in *his* place—the Word was made flesh (John 1:14)— and which precisely in this place lays claim to him. This is a place which in every instance and in every respect is laden with sin and guilt, no matter whether it be a royal throne, the parlour of a respectable citizen or a miserable hovel. It is a place which is of this world. This visitation of man by grace occurred in the incarnation of Jesus Christ, and it occurs in the word of Jesus Christ which is brought by the Holy Ghost. The call comes to man as a Gentile or as a Jew, free man or slave, man or woman, married or single. At the precise place where he is he is to hear the call and to allow it to lay claim to him. This does not mean that servitude or marriage or celibacy in itself is thereby justified; but the man who has been called can in any of these places belong to God. It is only through the call which I have heard in Christ, the call of the grace which lays claim to me, that, as a slave or as a free man, married or celibate, I can live justified before God. From the standpoint of Christ this life is now my calling; from my own standpoint it is my responsibility.

 . . . The calling is the call of Jesus Christ to belong wholly to Him; it is the laying claim to me by Christ at the place at which this call has found me; it embraces work with things and relations with persons; it demands a 'limited field of accomplishments', yet never as a value in itself, but in responsibility towards Jesus Christ. Through this relation to Christ the 'limited field of accomplishments' is freed from its isolation. Its boundary is broken through not only from above, that is to say by Christ, but also in an outward direction.

The Image of Christ

"WHOM HE foreknew, he also foreordained to be conformed to the image of his Son, that he might be the firstborn among many brethren" (Rom. 8:29). Here is a promise which passes all understanding. Those who follow Christ are destined to bear his image, and to be the brethren of the firstborn Son of God. Their goal is to become "as Christ." Christ's followers always have his image before their eyes, and in its light all other images are screened from their sight. It penetrates into the depths of their being, fills them, and makes them more and more like their Master. The image of Jesus Christ impresses itself in daily communion on the image of the disciple. No follower of Jesus can contemplate his image in a spirit of cold detachment. That image has the power to transform our lives, and if we surrender ourselves utterly to him, we cannot help bearing his image ourselves. We become the sons of God, we stand side by side with Christ, our unseen Brother, bearing like him the image of God.

Discipleship and the Cross

THE CROSS is laid on every Christian. The first Christ-suffering which every man must experience is the call to abandon the attachments of this world. It is that dying of the old man which is the result of his encounter with Christ. As we embark upon discipleship we surrender ourselves to Christ in union with his death—we give over our lives to death. Thus it begins; the cross is not the terrible end to an otherwise god-fearing and happy life, but it meets us at the beginning of our communion with Christ. When Christ calls a man, he bids him come and die. It may be a death like that of the first disciples who had to leave home and work to follow him, or it may be a death like Luther's, who had to leave the monastery and go out into the world. But it is the same death every time—death in Jesus Christ, the death of the old man at his call. Jesus' summons to the rich young man was calling him to die, because only the man who is dead to his own will can follow Christ. In fact every command of Jesus is a call to die, with all our affections and lusts. But we do not want to die, and therefore Jesus Christ and his call are necessarily our death as well as our life. The call to discipleship, the baptism in the name of Jesus Christ means both death and life. The call of Christ, his baptism, sets the Christian in the middle of the daily arena against sin and the devil. Every day he encounters new temptations, and every day he must suffer anew for Jesus Christ's sake. The wounds and scars he receives in the fray are living tokens of this participation in the cross of his Lord.

Christ Alone

THE LIFE of discipleship can only be maintained so long as nothing is allowed to come between Christ and ourselves—neither the law, nor personal piety, nor even the world. The disciple always looks only to his master, never to Christ *and* the law, Christ *and* religion, Christ *and* the world. He avoids all such notions like the plague. Only by following Christ alone can he preserve a single eye. His eye rests wholly on the light that comes from Christ, and has no darkness or ambiguity in it. As the eye must be single, clear and pure in order to keep light in the body, as hand and foot can receive light from no other source save the eye, as the foot stumbles and the hand misses its mark when the eye is dim, as the whole body is in darkness when the eye is blind; so the follower of Christ is in the light only so long as he looks simply to Christ and at nothing else in the world. Thus the heart of the disciple must be set upon Christ alone. If the eye sees an object which is not there, the whole body is deceived. If the heart is devoted to the mirage of the world, to the creature instead of the Creator, the disciple is lost.

Worldly possessions tend to turn the hearts of the disciples away from Jesus. What are we really devoted to? That is the question. Are our hearts set on earthly goods? Do we try to combine devotion to them with loyalty to Christ? Or are we devoted exclusively to him? The light of the body is the eye, and the light of the Christian is his heart. If the eye be dark, how great is the darkness of the body! But the heart is dark when it clings to earthly goods, for then, however urgently Jesus may call us, his call fails to find access to our hearts. Our hearts are closed, for they have already been given to another. As the light cannot penetrate the body when the eye is evil, so the word of Jesus cannot penetrate the disciple's heart so long as it is closed against it. The word is choked like the seed which was sown among thorns, choked "with cares and riches and pleasures of this life" (Luke 8:14).

The singleness of the eye and heart corresponds to that "hiddenness" which knows nothing but the call and word of Christ, and which consists in perfect fellowship with him. How can the disciple have dealings with earthly goods and yet preserve this singleness of heart? Jesus does not forbid the possession of property in itself. He was man, he ate and drank like his disciples, and thereby sanctified the good things of life. These necessities, which are consumed in use and which meet the legitimate requirements of the body, are to be used by the disciple with thankfulness.

Fellowship

THE FELLOWSHIP between Jesus and his disciples covered every aspect of their daily life. Within the fellowship of Christ's disciples the life of each individual was part of the life of the brotherhood. This common life bears living testimony to the concrete humanity of the Son of God. The bodily presence of God demands that for him and with him man should stake his own life in his daily existence. With all the concreteness of his bodily existence, man belongs to him who for his sake took upon him the human body. In the Christian life the individual disciple and the body of Jesus belong inseparably together.

All this is confirmed in the earliest record of the life of the Church in the Acts of the Apostles (Acts 2:42 ff; 4:32 ff). "They continued steadfastly in the apostles' teaching and fellowship, in the breaking of bread and the prayers."— "They that believed were of one heart and soul and...had all things in common." It is instructive to note that the fellowship (κοινωνία) is mentioned between Word and Sacrament. This is no accident, for fellowship always springs from the Word and finds its goal and completion in the Lord's Supper. The whole common life of the Christian fellowship oscillates between Word and Sacrament, it begins and ends in worship. It looks forward in expectation to the final banquet in the kingdom of God. When a community has such a source and goal it is a perfect communion of fellowship, in which even material goods fall into their appointed place. In freedom, joy and the power of the Holy Spirit a pattern of common life is produced where "neither was there among them any that lacked," where "distribution was made unto each according as anyone had need," where "not one of them said that aught of the things which he possessed was his own." In the everyday quality of these events we see a perfect picture of that evangelical liberty where there is no need of compulsion. They were indeed "of one heart and soul."

The Work

THESE TWELVE Jesus sent forth, and charged them, saying, Go not into any way of the Gentiles, and enter not into any city of the Samaritans; but go rather to the lost sheep of the house of Israel. (Matt. 10:5, 6)

All the activity of the disciples is subject to the clear precept of their Lord. They are not left free to choose their own methods or adopt their own conception of their task. Their work is to be Christ-work, and therefore they are absolutely dependent on the will of Jesus. Happy are they whose duty is fixed by such a precept, and who are therefore free from the tyranny of their own ideas and calculations.

In his very first word Jesus lays down a limitation of their work, a circumstance which they must inevitably have found strange and difficult. The choice of field for their labours does not depend on their own impulses or inclinations, but on where they are sent. This makes it quite clear that it is not their own work they are doing, but God's. How much they would have liked to go to the heathen and the Samaritans, who needed the glad tidings far more than anyone else. That may be quite true, but they receive no injunctions to go to them. The work of God cannot be done without due authorization, otherwise it is devoid of promise. Does it therefore follow that the promise and commission are not universally valid? Both are valid only where God authorizes them. But does not the very love of Christ constrain us to set no limit to its proclamation? The love of Jesus is something very different from our own zeal and enthusiasms because it adheres to its mission. What is the urge which drives us to proclaim the saving truths of the gospel? It is not just love for our fellow-countrymen or for the heathen in foreign lands: it is the Lord's commission as he delivered it in his missionary charge. It is only that commission which can show us the place where the promise lies. If Christ will not let us preach the gospel in any particular place, we must give up the attempt and abide by his will and word. Thus the disciples are bound to the word and to the terms of their commission. They can only go where the word of Christ and his commission direct them, "Go not into any way of the Gentiles, and enter not into any city of the Samaritans; but go rather to the lost sheep of the house of Israel."

'The Harvest Is Great'

..."FEED MY LAMBS" was the last charge Jesus gave to Peter. The Good Shepherd protects his sheep against the wolf, and instead of fleeing he gives his life for the sheep. He knows them all by name and loves them. He knows their distress and their weakness. He heals the wounded, gives drink to the thirsty, sets upright the falling, and leads them gently, not sternly, to pasture. He leads them on the right way. He seeks the one lost sheep, and brings it back to the fold. But the bad shepherds lord it over the flock by force, forgetting their charges and pursuing their own interests. Jesus is looking for good shepherds, and there are none to be found.

The prospect grips his heart, and his divine pity goes out to this erring flock, these multitudes who surge around him. From the human point of view everything looks hopeless, but Jesus sees things with different eyes. Instead of the people maltreated, wretched and poor, he sees the ripe harvest field of God. "The harvest is great." It is ripe enough to be gathered into the barns. The hour has come for these poor and wretched folk to be fetched home to the kingdom of God. Jesus beholds the promise of God descending on the multitudes where the scribes and zealots saw only a field trampled down, burnt and ravaged. Jesus sees the fields waving with corn and ripe for the kingdom of God. The harvest is great, but only Jesus in his mercy can see it.

There is now no time to lose: the work of harvest brooks no delay. "But the labourers are few." It is hardly surprising that so few are granted to see things with the pitying eyes of Jesus, for only those who share the love of his heart have been given eyes to see. And only they can enter the harvest field.

Jesus is looking for help, for he cannot do the work alone. Who will come forward to help him and work with him? Only God knows, and he must give them to his Son. No man dare presume to come forward and offer himself on his own initiative, not even the disciples themselves. Their duty is to pray the Lord of the harvest to send forth labourers at the right moment, for the time is ripe.

The Fruit

HE THAT RECEIVETH YOU receiveth me, and he that receiveth me receiveth him that sent me. He that receiveth a prophet in the name of a prophet shall receive a prophet's reward; and he that receiveth a righteous man in the name of a righteous man shall receive a righteous man's reward. And whosoever shall give to drink unto one of these little ones a cup of cold water only, in the name of a disciple, verily I say unto you, he shall in no wise lose his reward. (Matt. 10:40–42)

The bearers of Jesus' word receive a final word of promise for their work. They are now Christ's fellow-workers, and will be like him in all things. Thus they are to meet those to whom they are sent as if they were Christ himself. When they are welcomed into a house, Christ enters with them. They are bearers of his presence. They bring with them the most precious gift in the world, the gift of Jesus Christ. And with him they bring God the Father, and that means indeed forgiveness and salvation, life and bliss. That is the reward and fruit of their toil and suffering. Every service men render them is service rendered to Christ himself. This means grace for the Church and grace for the disciple in equal measure. The Church will be readier to give them its service and honour for with them the Lord himself has entered into their midst. But the disciples are given to understand that when they enter into a house they do not enter in vain. They bring with them an incomparable gift. It is a law of the kingdom of God that every man shall participate in the gift which he willingly receives as a gift from God. The man who receives a prophet and knows what he is doing will participate in the prophet's cause, his gift and his reward. He who receives a righteous man will receive the reward of a righteous man, for he has become a partner in his righteousness. He who offers a cup of cold water to the weakest and poorest who bears no honourable name has ministered to Christ himself, and Jesus Christ will be his reward.

Thus the disciples are bidden lastly to think, not about their own way, their own sufferings and their own reward, but of the goal of their labours, which is the salvation of the Church.

The Ministry of Helpfulness

WE MUST BE READY to allow ourselves to be interrupted by God. God will be constantly crossing our paths and canceling our plans by sending us people with claims and petitions. We may pass them by, preoccupied with our more important tasks, as the priest passed by the man who had fallen among thieves, perhaps—reading the Bible. When we do that we pass by the visible sign of the Cross raised athwart our path to show us that, not our way, but God's way must be done. It is a strange fact that Christians and even ministers frequently consider their work so important and urgent that they will allow nothing to disturb them. They think they are doing God a service in this, but actually they are disdaining God's "crooked yet straight path" (Gottfried Arnold). They do not want a life that is crossed and balked. But it is part of the discipline of humility that we must not spare our hand where it can perform a service and that we do not assume that our schedule is our own to manage, but allow it to be arranged by God.

Fulfilling Our Tasks

...I THINK WE MUST RISE to the great demands that are made on us personally, and yet at the same time fulfil the commonplace and necessary tasks of daily life. We must confront fate—to me the neuter gender of the word 'fate' (*Schicksal*) is significant—as resolutely as we submit to it at the right time. One can speak of 'guidance' only on the other side of that twofold process, with God meeting us no longer as 'Thou', but also 'disguised' in the 'It'; so in the last resort my question is how we are to find the 'Thou' in this 'It' (i.e. fate), or, in other words, how does 'fate' really become 'guidance'? It's therefore impossible to define the boundary between resistance and submission on abstract principles; but both of them must exist, and both must be practised. Faith demands this elasticity of behaviour. Only so can we stand our ground in each situation as it arises, and turn it to gain.

The Sermon on the Mount

EVERY ONE THEREFORE which heareth these words of mine, and doeth them, shall be likened unto a wise man, which built his house upon the rock: and the rain descended, and the floods came, and the winds blew, and beat upon that house; and it fell not: for it was founded upon the rock. And every one that heareth these words of mine, and doeth them not, shall be likened unto a foolish man, which built his house upon the sand: and the rain descended, and the floods came, and the winds blew, and smote upon that house; and it fell: and great was the fall thereof.

And it came to pass, when Jesus ended these words, the multitudes were astonished at his teaching: for he taught them as one having authority, and not as their scribes. (Matt. 7:24–29)

We have listened to the Sermon on the Mount and perhaps have understood it. But who has heard it aright? Jesus gives the answer at the end. He does not allow his hearers to go away and make of his sayings what they will, picking and choosing from them whatever they find helpful, and testing them to see if they work. He does not give them free rein to misuse his word with their mercenary hands, but gives it to them on condition that it retains exclusive power over them. Humanly speaking, we could understand and interpret the Sermon on the Mount in a thousand different ways. Jesus knows only one possibility: simple surrender and obedience, not interpreting it or applying it, but doing and obeying it. That is the only way to hear his word. But again he does not mean that it is to be discussed as an ideal, he really means us to get on with it.

This word, whose claim we recognize, this word which issues from his saying "I have known thee," this word which sets us at once to work and obedience, is the rock on which to build our house. The only proper response to this word which Jesus brings with him from eternity is simply to do it. Jesus has spoken: his is the word, ours the obedience. Only in the doing of it does the word of Jesus retain its honour, might and power among us. Now the storm can rage over the house, but it cannot shatter that union with him, which his word has created.

Visionary Dreaming

GOD HATES visionary dreaming; it makes the dreamer proud and pretentious. The man who fashions a visionary ideal of community demands that it be realized by God, by others, and by himself. He enters the community of Christians with his demands, sets up his own law, and judges the brethren and God Himself accordingly. He stands adamant, a living reproach to all others in the circle of brethren. He acts as if he is the creator of the Christian community, as if his dream binds men together. When things do not go his way, he calls the effort a failure. When his ideal picture is destroyed, he sees the community going to smash. So he becomes, first an accuser of his brethren, then an accuser of God, and finally the despairing accuser of himself.

Because God has already laid the only foundation of our fellowship, because God has bound us together in one body with other Christians in Jesus Christ, long before we entered into common life with them, we enter into that common life not as demanders but as thankful recipients. We thank God for what He has done for us. We thank God for giving us brethren who live by His call, by His forgiveness, and His promise. We do not complain of what God does not give us; we rather thank God for what He does give us daily. . . .

Christian Radicalism

RADICALISM ALWAYS SPRINGS from a conscious or unconscious hatred of what is established. Christian radicalism, no matter whether it consists in withdrawing from the world or in improving the world, arises from hatred of creation. The radical cannot forgive God His creation. He has fallen out with the created world, the Ivan Karamazov, who at the same time makes the figure of the radical Jesus in the legend of the Grand Inquisitor. When evil becomes powerful in the world, it infects the Christian, too, with the poison of radicalism. It is Christ's gift to the Christian that he should be reconciled with the world as it is, but now this reconciliation is accounted a betrayal and denial of Christ. It is replaced by bitterness, suspicion and contempt for men and the world. In the place of the love that believes all, bears all and hopes all, in the place of the love which loves the world in its very wickedness with the love of God (John 3:16), there is now the pharisaical denial of love to evil, and the restriction of love to the closed circle of the devout. Instead of the open Church of Jesus Christ, which serves the world till the end, there is now some allegedly primitive Christian ideal of a Church, which in its turn confuses the reality of the living Jesus Christ with the realization of a Christian idea. Thus a world which has become evil succeeds in making the Christians become evil too. It is the same germ that disintegrates the world and that makes the Christians become radical. In both cases it is hatred towards the world, no matter whether the haters are the ungodly or the godly. On both sides it is a refusal of faith in the creation. But devils are not cast out through Beelzebub.

Human Relationships

...THERE IS HARDLY ANYTHING that can make one happier than to feel that one counts for something with other people. What matters here is not numbers, but intensity. In the long run, human relationships are the most important thing in life; the modern 'efficient' man can do nothing to change this, nor can the demigods and lunatics who know nothing about human relationships. God uses us in his dealings with others.

The Friend

NOT from the heavy soil,
where blood and sex and oath
rule in their hallowed might,
where earth itself,
guarding the primal consecrated order,
avenges wantonness and madness—
not from the heavy soil of earth,
but from the spirit's choice and free desire,
needing no oath or legal bond,
is friend bestowed on friend.

Beside the cornfield that sustains us,
tilled and cared for reverently by men
sweating as they labour at their task,
and, if need be, giving their life's blood—
beside the field that gives their daily bread
men also let the lovely cornflower thrive.
No one has planted, no one watered it;
it grows, defenceless and in freedom,
and in glad confidence of life untroubled
under the open sky.
Beside the staff of life,
taken and fashioned from the heavy earth,
beside our marriage, work, and war,
the free man, too, will live and grow towards the sun.
Not the ripe fruit alone—
blossom is lovely, too.
Does blossom only serve the fruit,

or does fruit only serve the blossom—
who knows?
But both are given to us.
Finest and rarest blossom,
at a happy moment springing
from the freedom of a lightsome, daring, trusting
    spirit,
is a friend to a friend.

Playmates at first
on the spirit's long journeys
to distant and wonderful realms
that, veiled by the morning sunlight,
glitter like gold;
when, in the midday heat
the gossamer clouds in the deep blue sky
drift slowly towards them—
realms that, when night stirs the senses,
lit by the lamps in the darkness,
like treasures prudently hidden
beckon the seeker.

When the spirit touches
man's heart and brow
with thoughts that are lofty, bold, serene,
so that with clear eyes he will face the world
as a free man may;
when then the spirit gives birth to action
by which alone we stand or fall;
when from the sane and resolute action
rises the work that gives a man's life
content and meaning—
then would that man,
lonely and actively working,
know of the spirit that grasps and befriends him,
like waters clear and refreshing

where the spirit is cleansed from the dust
and cooled from the heat that oppressed him,
steeling himself in the hour of fatigue—
like a fortress to which, from confusion and danger,
the spirit returns,
wherein he finds refuge and comfort and
    strengthening,
is a friend to a friend.

And the spirit will trust,
trust without limit.

Sickened by vermin
that feed, in the shade of the good,
on envy, greed, and suspicion,
by the snake-like hissing
of venomous tongues
that fear and hate and revile
the mystery of free thought
and upright heart,
the spirit would cast aside all deceit,
open his heart to the spirit he trusts,
and unite with him freely as one.
Ungrudging, he will support,
will thank and acknowledge him,
and from him draw happiness and strength.

But always to rigorous
judgment and censure
freely assenting,
man seeks, in his manhood,
not orders, not laws and peremptory dogmas,
but counsel from one who is earnest in goodness
and faithful in friendship,
making man free.

Distant or near,
in joy or in sorrow,
each in the other
sees his true helper
to brotherly freedom.

At midnight came the air-raid siren's song;
I thought of you in silence and for long—
how you are faring, how our lives once were,
and how I wish you home this coming year.

We wait till half past one, and hear at last
the signal that the danger now is past;
so danger—if the omen does not lie—
of every kind shall gently pass you by.

Life Together

...IT IS NOT simply to be taken for granted that the Christian has the privilege of living among other Christians. Jesus Christ lived in the midst of his enemies. At the end all his disciples deserted him. On the Cross he was utterly alone, surrounded by evildoers and mockers. For this cause he had come, to bring peace to the enemies of God. So the Christian, too, belongs not in the seclusion of a cloistered life but in the thick of foes. There is his commission, his work....

The Joy of Fellowship

...THE PRISONER, the sick person, the Christian in exile sees in the companionship of a fellow Christian a physical sign of the gracious presence of the triune God. Visitor and visited in loneliness recognize in each other the Christ who is present in the body; they receive and meet each other as one meets the Lord, in reverence, humility, and joy. They receive each other's benedictions as the benediction of the Lord Jesus Christ. But if there is so much blessing and joy even in a single encounter of brother with brother, how inexhaustible are the riches that open up for those who by God's will are privileged to live in the daily fellowship of life with other Christians!

It is true, of course, that what is an unspeakable gift of

God for the lonely individual is easily disregarded and trodden under foot by those who have the gift every day. It is easily forgotten that the fellowship of Christian brethren is a gift of grace, a gift of the Kingdom of God that any day may be taken from us, that the time that still separates us from utter loneliness may be brief indeed. Therefore, let him who until now has had the privilege of living a common Christian life with other Christians praise God's grace from the bottom of his heart. Let him thank God on his knees and declare: It is grace, nothing but grace, that we are allowed to live in community with Christian brethren.

Love

...THE REVELATION OF GOD is Jesus Christ. 'In this was manifested the love of God toward us, because that God sent his only begotten Son into the world, that we might live through him' (I John 4:9). God's revelation in Jesus Christ, God's revelation of His love, precedes all our love towards Him. Love has its origin not in us but in God. Love is not an attitude of men but an attitude of God. 'Herein is love, not that we loved God, but that he loved us, and sent his Son to be the propitiation for our sins' (I John 4:10). Only in Jesus Christ do we know what love is, namely, in His deed for us. 'Hereby perceive we the love of God, because he laid down his life for us' (I John 3:16). And even here there is given no general definition of love, in the sense, for example, of its being the laying down of one's life for the lives of others. What is here called love is not this general principle but the utterly unique event of the laying down of the life of Jesus Christ for us. Love is inseparably bound up with the name of Jesus Christ as the revelation of God. The New Testament answers the question 'What is love?' quite unambiguously by pointing solely and entirely to Jesus Christ. He is the only definition of love. But again it would be a complete misunderstanding if we were to derive a general definition of love from our view of Jesus Christ and of His deed and His suffering. Love is not what He *does* and what He *suffers*, but it is what *He* does and what *He* suffers. Love is always He Himself. Love is always God Himself. Love is always the revelation of God in Jesus Christ.

The Strength of the Other Person

"It is not good that the man should be alone; I will make him a helper fit for him."

THE FIRST MAN is alone. Christ was also alone. And we are alone as well. Everyone is alone in his own way: Adam is alone in the expectation of the other person, the community. Christ is alone because only he loves the other person, because he is the way by which mankind has returned to its Creator. We are alone because we have pushed the other person from us, because we hated him. Adam was alone in hope, Christ was alone in the fullness of deity, and we are alone in evil, in hopelessness.

God creates a companion, a helpmeet, for Adam. It is not good that Adam is alone. For what purpose does man, living in the protection of God, need a companion? The answer is only revealed if we consider the story in its context again and again. In the Bible otherwise only God is a companion, a helpmeet to man. So if woman is here spoken of in this way it must mean something quite unusual. This follows from the description. First of all God forms animals out of the ground from which he formed man. According to the Bible men and animals have the same bodies! Perhaps he may find a companion among these brothers, for the animals really are of the same origin as he. The peculiar feature of this is that man must obviously know for himself whether these animals can be companions for him or not. Adam's companion was to be whichever creature he called his companion as the creatures were brought before him. There is Adam, the intelligent, calling all the animals by name—the brotherly world of the animals who have been taken from the same ground as he—and letting them pass by him. It was his first pain that these brothers whom he loved did not fulfill his own expectations: they remained a strange world to him. Indeed, in all good fellowship, they remain creatures subjected to him, whom he names and over which he rules. Adam remains alone. As far as I know, nowhere else in the history of religions have the animals been spoken of in such a significant context. When God desires to create for man, in the form of another creature, the helper he is himself, in the first place the animals are created; they are named and set in their places. Still Adam is alone. That which came out of the ground remains a stranger to him.

Marriage

...MARRIAGE IS THE UNION of two human beings as human beings, on the basis of the free decision of the individual. So long as human nature continues, it will continue to lay claim to this right. The denial of this right for any reason which lies neither on the entirely individual plane nor on the general human plane will sooner or later always prove ineffectual in the face of the power of natural life. The right of men and women to a child of their own, which implies the right to the choice of a partner in marriage, can never, in the long run, be overruled by considerations of class or of religious outlook or on economic or biological grounds. The human will to reproduce can never be interpreted as a purely social, economic, religious or biological obligation. All these factors may, and indeed must, be considered in making one's own choice, but they cannot replace the free decision. In marriage an individual unites himself with an individual, a human being with a human being. Economic, denominational, social and national ties all contribute to determining the decision of the individual, but they can neither obviate nor anticipate this decision. The reason for this lies in the fact that the desire for a child of one's own and the free choice of a mate which this implies, in other words human marriage, is the oldest of all human institutions and cannot therefore be conditional upon these secondary factors.

Human marriage existed before the development of any of the other bonds of human society. Marriage was given already with the creation of the first man. Its right is founded in the beginnings of mankind.

The Community of Love

Therefore a man leaves his father and his mother and cleaves to his wife, and they become one flesh.

IT COULD BE SAID that here the narrator is obviously stumbling. How can Adam, who knows nothing of a father or a mother, say such a thing? We could also say this is the narrator's practical application of the story, or something of the kind. Really, though, we recognize a basic fact here which has so far been hidden and which has now, as it were unintentionally, come to light. We ourselves are the Adam who speaks. We have a father and a mother and we know the uniqueness of belonging to one another in the love of man and woman, but for us this knowledge has been wholly spoilt and destroyed by our guilt. This passage does not justify running away from the worldly order or from our connexion with our father and mother. It is the profoundest way possible of describing the depth and seriousness of belonging to one another. This ultimate belonging to one another is undoubtedly seen here in connexion with man's sexuality. Very clearly sexuality is the expression of the two-sidedness of being both an individual and being one with the other person. Sexuality is nothing but the ultimate realization of our belonging to one another. Here sexuality has as yet no life of its own detached from this purpose. Here the community of man and woman is the community derived from God, the community of love glorifying and worshipping him as the Creator.

Christ the Foundation

God gives you Christ as the foundation of your marriage. 'Welcome one another, therefore, as Christ has welcomed you, for the glory of God' (Rom. 15[7]). In a word, live together in the forgiveness of your sins, for without it no human fellowship, least of all a marriage, can survive. Don't insist on your rights, don't blame each other, don't judge or condemn each other, don't find fault with each other, but accept each other as you are, and forgive each other every day from the bottom of your hearts.

What God Has Joined Together

God is guiding your marriage. Marriage is more than your love for each other. It has a higher dignity and power, for it is God's holy ordinance, through which he wills to perpetuate the human race till the end of time. In your love you see only your two selves in the world, but in marriage you are a link in the chain of the generations, which God causes to come and to pass away to his glory, and calls into his kingdom. In your love you see only the heaven of your own happiness, but in marriage you are placed at a post of responsibility towards the world and mankind. Your love is your own private possession, but marriage is more than something personal—it is a status, an office. Just as it is the crown, and not merely the will to rule, that makes the king, so it is marriage, and not merely your love for each other, that joins you together in the sight of God and man. As you first gave the ring to one another and have now received it a second time from the hand of the pastor, so love comes from you, but marriage from above, from God. As high as God is above man, so high are the sanctity, the rights, and the promise of marriage above the sanctity, the rights, and the promise of love. It is not your love that sustains the marriage, but from now on, the marriage that sustains your love.

God makes your marriage indissoluble. 'What therefore God has joined together, let no man put asunder' (Matt. 19:6). God joins you together in marriage; it is his act, not yours. Do not confound your love for one another with God. God makes your marriage indissoluble, and protects it from every danger that may threaten it from within and without; he wills to be the guarantor of its indissolubility. It is a blessed thing to know that no power on earth, no temptation, no human frailty can dissolve what God holds together; indeed, anyone who knows that may say confidently: What God has joined together, *can* no man put asunder. Free from all the anxiety that is always a characteristic of love, you can now say to each other with complete and confident assurance: We can never lose each other now; by the will of God we belong to each other till death.

Home

THE HOMES OF MEN are not, like the shelters of animals, merely the means of protection against bad weather and the night or merely places for rearing the young; they are places in which a man may relish the joys of his personal life in the intimacy and security of his family and of his property. Eating and drinking do not merely serve the purpose of keeping the body in good health, but they afford natural joy in bodily living. Clothing is not intended merely as a mean covering for the body, but also as an adornment of the body. Recreation is not designed solely to increase working efficiency, but it provides the body with its due measure of repose and enjoyment. Play is by its nature remote from all subordination to purpose, and it thus demonstrates most clearly that the life of the body is an end in itself. Sex is not only the means of reproduction, but, independently of this defined purpose, it brings with it its own joy, in married life, in the love of two human beings for one another. From all this it emerges that the meaning of bodily life never lies solely in its subordination to its final purpose. The life of the body assumes its full significance only with the fulfilment of its inherent claim to joy.

The Security of Home

IN THE REVOLUTIONARY TIMES ahead the greatest gift will be to know the security of a good home. It will be a bulwark against all dangers from within and without. The time when children broke away in arrogance from their parents will be past. Children will be drawn into their parents' protection, and they will seek refuge, counsel, peace, and enlightenment. You are lucky to have parents who know at first hand what it means to have a parental home in stormy times. In the general impoverishment of intellectual life you will find your parents' home a storehouse of spiritual values and a source of intellectual stimulation. Music, as your parents understand and practise it, will help to dissolve your perplexities and purify your character and sensibility, and in times of care and sorrow will keep a ground-bass of joy alive in you. Your parents will soon be teaching you to help yourself and never to be afraid of soiling your hands. The piety of your home will not be noisy or loquacious, but it will teach you to say your prayers, to fear and love God above everything, and to do the will of Jesus Christ. 'My son, keep your father's commandment, and forsake not your mother's teaching. Bind them upon your heart always; tie them about your neck. When you walk, they will lead you; when you lie down, they will watch over you; and when you awake, they will talk with you' (Prov. 6:20–22). 'Today salvation has come to this house' (Luke 19:9).

A Virtuous Woman

THE PLACE where God has put the wife is the husband's home. Most people have forgotten nowadays what a home can mean, though some of us have come to realize it as never before. It is a kingdom of its own in the midst of the world, a stronghold amid life's storms and stresses, a refuge, even a sanctuary. It is not founded on the shifting sands of outward or public life, but it has its peace in God, for it is God who gives it its special meaning and value, its own nature and privilege, its own destiny and dignity. It is an ordinance of God in the world, the place in which— whatever may happen in the world—peace, quietness, joy, love, purity, discipline, respect, obedience, tradition, and, with it all, happiness may dwell. It is the wife's calling, and her happiness, to build up for her husband this world within the world, and to do her life's work there. How happy she is if she realizes how great and rich a task and destiny she has. Not novelty, but permanence; not change, but constancy; not noisiness, but peace; not words, but deeds; not commands, but persuasion; not desire, but possession—and all these things inspired and sustained by her love for her husband—, that is the wife's kingdom. In the Book of Proverbs we read [31:11ff.]: 'The heart of her husband trusts in her, and he will have no lack of gain. She does him good, and not harm, all the days of her life. She seeks wool and flax, and works with willing hands.... She rises while it is yet night and provides food for her household and tasks for her maidens.... She opens her hand to the poor, and reaches out her hands to the needy...Strength and dignity are her clothing, and she laughs at the time to come...Her children rise up and call her blessed; her husband also, and he praises her...Many women have done excellently, but you surpass them all.' Again and again the Bible praises, as the supreme earthly happiness, the fortune of a man who finds a true, or as the Bible puts it, a 'virtuous' or 'wise' woman. 'She is far more precious than jewels' [Prov. 31:10]. 'A virtuous woman is the crown of her husband' [Prov. 12:4]....

To His Mother

[Prinz-Albrecht-Strasse]
28 December 1944

Dear mother,
I'm so glad to have just got permission to write you a birthday letter. I have to write in some haste, as the post is just going. All I really want to do is to help to cheer you a little in these days that you must be finding so bleak. Dear mother, I want you to know that I am constantly thinking of you and father every day, and that I thank God for all that you are to me and the whole family. I know you've always lived for us and haven't lived a life of your own. That is why you're the only one with whom I can share all that I'm going through. It's a very great comfort to me that Maria is with you. Thank you for all the love that has come to me in my cell from you during the past year, and has made every day easier for me. I think these hard years have brought us closer together than we ever were before. My wish for you and father and Maria and for us all is that the New Year may bring us at least an occasional glimmer of light, and that we may once more have the joy of being together. May God keep you both well.

With most loving wishes, dear, dear mother, for a happy birthday.

Your grateful Dietrich

The Heritage of Children

God has laid on marriage a blessing and a burden. The blessing is
the promise of children. God allows man to share in his
continual work of creation; but it is always God himself
who blesses marriage with children. 'Children are a heritage from the Lord' (Ps. 127:3), and they should be acknowledged as such. It is from God that parents receive
their children, and it is to God that they should lead them.
Parents therefore have divine authority in respect of their
children. Luther speaks of the 'golden chain' with which
God invests parents; and scripture adds to the fifth commandment the special promise of long life on earth. Since
men live on earth, God has given them a lasting reminder
that this earth stands under the curse of sin and is not itself
the ultimate reality. Over the destiny of woman and of man
lies the dark shadow of a word of God's wrath, a burden
from God, which they must carry. The woman must bear
her children in pain, and in providing for his family the
man must reap many thorns and thistles, and labour in the
sweat of his brow. This burden should cause both man and
wife to call on God, and should remind them of their eternal
destiny in his kingdom. Earthly society is only the beginning of the heavenly society, the earthly home an image of
the heavenly home, the earthly family a symbol of the
fatherhood of God over all men, for they are his children.

Abortion

MARRIAGE INVOLVES acknowledgement of the right of life that is to come into being, a right which is not subject to the disposal of the married couple. Unless this right is acknowledged as a matter of principle, marriage ceases to be marriage and becomes a mere liaison. Acknowledgement of this right means making way for the free creative power of God which can cause new life to proceed from this marriage according to His will. Destruction of the embryo in the mother's womb is a violation of the right to live which God has bestowed upon this nascent life. To raise the question whether we are here concerned already with a human being or not is merely to confuse the issue. The simple fact is that God certainly intended to create a human being and that this nascent human being has been deliberately deprived of his life. And that is nothing but murder. A great many different motives may lead to an action of this kind; indeed in cases where it is an act of despair, performed in circumstances of extreme human or economic destitution and misery, the guilt may often lie rather with the community than with the individual. Precisely in this connexion money may conceal many a wanton deed, while the poor man's more reluctant lapse may far more easily be disclosed. All these considerations must no doubt have a quite decisive influence on our personal and pastoral attitude towards the person concerned, but they cannot in any way alter the fact of murder.[1]

---

[1]In view of the general practice serious thought must be provoked by the strong disapproval which the Roman Catholic Church expresses with regard to

the killing of the foetus in cases where the mother is in danger of losing her life. If the child has its right to life from God, and is perhaps already capable of life, then the killing of the child, as an alternative to the presumed natural death of the mother, is surely a highly questionable action. The life of the mother is in the hand of God, but the life of the child is arbitrarily extinguished. The question whether the life of the mother or the life of the child is of greater value can hardly be a matter for a human decision.

The Rights of Natural Life

...GOD'S HAVING CREATED the individual, and His having called him to eternal life, is a reality which is operative in natural life, and a reality which it is extremely dangerous to neglect. Within natural life, therefore, it is incumbent upon reason to take account of the right of the individual, even though the divine origin of this right is not recognized. Consequently the natural enemy of social eudemonism has always been reason, the organ which 'perceives' and introduces into consciousness the reality of the fallen world. Social eudemonism, for its part, allies itself with a blind voluntarism in an 'irrational', inconceivable overestimation of the power of the will in its encounter with the reality of natural life itself. It is a truth which lies beyond the reach of this voluntarism that reason is closer to reality than is the blind will, even though this blind will may claim to be closer to reality than anything else can be. The principle of *suum cuique* is the highest possible attainment of a reason which is in accord with reality and which, within the natural life, discerns the right which is given to the individual by God (of whom reason knows nothing).

In our discussion of the rights of natural life from the point of view of their contents the question of the guarantor of these rights will repeatedly demand an answer. Who is it that supports the rights of natural life with an effective guarantee? Here we must repeat what we have said already. It is in the first place God Himself who guarantees these rights. But for this purpose He continually makes use of life itself, which sooner or later gains the upper hand in spite of every violation of the natural. We have to reckon here with periods of time which may extend beyond the life span of the individual. The reason for this is that in the domain of natural life what matters is not so much the individual as the preservation of the life of man as a species. Natural life necessarily often rides rough-shod over the individual. If the right of the individual is destroyed, and perhaps not restored, this will augment the power of resistance of natural life and enable it to reassert itself in the next or next but one generation. It is the problem of a theodicy that presents itself here, but the solution of this problem must await a later occasion. If it is God, and through Him life itself, that intervenes effectively on behalf of the rights that are inherent in life, then any action of which the individual is capable in defence of his natural rights can only be of extremely restricted significance. What the individual does, in fact, do will depend on a large number of considerations which at present lie beyond the scope of our enquiry. But in any case he will always have to bear in mind that his most powerful ally is life itself. If one asks whether the individual is entitled to defend his natural rights, then the answer must clearly be yes. But in all circumstances he must defend the right in such a manner as to carry the conviction that it is not the individual but God who guarantees it.

The Rights of Bodily Life

THE LIFE OF THE BODY, like life in general, is both a means to an end and an end in itself. To regard the body exclusively as a means to an end is idealistic but not Christian; for a means is discarded as soon as the end is achieved. It is from this point of view that the body is conceived as the prison from which the immortal soul is released for ever by death. According to the Christian doctrine, the body possesses a higher dignity. Man is a bodily being, and remains so in eternity as well. Bodiliness and human life belong inseparably together. And thus the bodiliness which is willed by God to be the form of existence of man is entitled to be called an end in itself. This does not exclude the fact that the body at the same time continues to be subordinated to a higher purpose. But what is important is that as one of the rights of bodily life its preservation is not only a means to an end but also an end in itself. It is in the joys of the body that it becomes apparent that the body is an end in itself within the natural life. If the body were only a means to an end man would have no right to bodily joys. It would then not be permissible to exceed an expedient minimum of bodily enjoyment. This would have very far-reaching consequences for the Christian appraisal of all the problems that have to do with the life of the body, housing, food, clothing, recreation, play and sex. But if the body is rightly to be regarded as an end in itself, then there is a right to bodily joys, even though these are not necessarily subordinated to some higher purpose. It is inherent in the nature of joy itself that it is spoilt by any thought of purpose. We shall have to return to this later on when we come to deal with the right to happiness. Within the natural life the joys of the body are reminders of the eternal joy which has been promised to men by God....

The Value of a Life

...THE IDEA OF DESTROYING a life which has lost its social usefulness is one which springs from weakness, not from strength.

But, above all, this idea springs from the false assumption that life consists only in its own usefulness to society. It is not perceived that life, created and preserved by God, possesses an inherent right which is wholly independent of its social utility. The right to live is a matter of the essence and not of any values. In the sight of God there is no life that is not worth living; for life itself is valued by God. The fact that God is the Creator, Preserver and Redeemer of life makes even the most wretched life worth living before God. The beggar Lazarus, a leper, lay at the rich man's gate and the dogs licked his sores; he was devoid of any social usefulness and a victim of those who judge life according to its social usefulness; yet God held him to be worthy of eternal life. And where if not in God should there lie the criterion for the ultimate value of a life? In the subjective will to live? On this rating many a genius is excelled by half-wits. In the judgement of society? If so it would soon be found that opinion as to which lives were socially valuable or valueless would be determined by the requirements of the moment and therefore by arbitrary decisions; one group of human beings after another would in this way be condemned to extermination. The distinction between life that is worth living and life that is not worth living must sooner or later destroy life itself. Now that we have made this principle clear, we must still say a word about the purely social utility of the seemingly useless and meaningless life. We cannot indeed ignore the fact that precisely the supposedly worthless life of the incurably sick evokes from the healthy, from doctors, nurses and relatives, the very highest measure of social self-sacrifice and even genuine heroism; this devoted service which is rendered by sound life to sick life has given rise to real values which are of the highest utility for the community.

Suicide

GOD, THE CREATOR and Lord of life, Himself exercises the right over life. Man does not need to lay hands upon himself in order to justify his life. And because he does not need to do this it follows that it is not rightful for him to do it. It is a remarkable fact that the Bible nowhere expressly forbids suicide, but that suicide appears there very often (though not always) as the consequence of extremely grave sin, so, for example, in the case of the traitors Ahithophel and Judas. The reason for this is not that the Bible sanctions suicide, but that, instead of prohibiting it, it desires to call the despairing to repentance and to mercy. A man who is on the brink of suicide no longer has ears for commands or prohibitions; all he can hear now is God's merciful summons to faith, to deliverance and to conversion. A man who is desperate cannot be saved by a law that appeals to his own strength; such a law will only drive him to even more hopeless despair. One who despairs of life can be helped only by the saving deed of another, the offer of a new life which is to be lived not by his own strength but by the grace of God. A man who can no longer live is not helped by any command that he should live, but only by a new spirit.

God maintains the right of life, even against the man who has grown tired of his life. He gives man freedom to pledge his life for something greater, but it is not His will that man should turn this freedom arbitrarily against his own life. Man must not lay hands upon himself, even though he must sacrifice his life for others. Even if his earthly life has become a torment for him, he must commit it intact into God's hand, from which it came, and he must not try to break free by his own efforts, for in dying he falls again into the hand of God, which he found too severe while he lived.

Fulfilment

ONLY THE TRIUMPHAL ENTRY of the Lord will bring with it the fulfilment of manhood and goodness. But a light is already shed by the coming Lord upon what is meant by being man and by being good in the way which is required for true preparation and expectation. It is only by reference to the Lord who is to come, and who has come, that we can know what it is to be man and to be good. It is because Christ is coming that we must be men and that we must be good. For Christ is not coming to hell, but to 'His own' (John 1:11); He is coming to His creation, which, in spite of its fall, is His creation still. Christ is not coming to devils but to men, certainly to men who are sinful, lost and damned, but still to men. That the fallen creation is still the creation, and that sinful man still remains man, follows from the fact that Christ is coming to them and that Christ redeems them from sin and from the power of the devil. It is in relation to Christ that the fallen world becomes intelligible as the world which is preserved and sustained by God for the coming of Christ, the world in which we can and should live good lives as men in orders which are established. But wherever man becomes a thing, a merchandise, a machine, wherever the established orders are arbitrarily destroyed, and wherever the distinction is lost between 'good' and 'evil', there the reception of Christ is impeded by an additional obstacle over and above the general sinfulness and forlornness of the world. There the world is destroying itself, so that it is in grave peril of becoming devilish. Even in the midst of the fallen, lost world, it makes a difference in God's sight whether a man observes or violates the order of marriage and whether he acts justly or arbitrarily. Certainly he is still a sinner, even though he is blameless in marriage and a protector of justice, but it still makes a difference whether the penultimate is attended to and taken seriously or not. The preparation of the way requires that the penultimate shall be respected and validated for the sake of the approaching ultimate.

Of Success

ALTHOUGH IT IS CERTAINLY NOT TRUE that success justifies an evil deed and shady means, it is impossible to regard success as something that is ethically quite neutral. The fact is that historical success creates a basis for the continuance of life, and it is still a moot point whether it is ethically more responsible to take the field like a Don Quixote against a new age, or to admit one's defeat, accept the new age, and agree to serve it. In the last resort success makes history; and the ruler of history repeatedly brings good out of evil over the heads of the history-makers. Simply to ignore the ethical significance of success is a short-circuit created by dogmatists who think unhistorically and irresponsibly; and it is good for us sometimes to be compelled to grapple seriously with the ethical problem of success. As long as goodness is successful, we can afford the luxury of regarding it as having no ethical significance; it is when success is achieved by evil means that the problem arises. In the face of such a situation we find that it cannot be adequately dealt with, either by theoretical dogmatic arm-chair criticism, which means a refusal to face the facts, or by opportunism, which means giving up the struggle and surrendering to success. We will not and must not be either outraged critics or opportunists, but must take our share of responsibility for the moulding of history in every situation and at every moment, whether we are the victors or the vanquished. One who will not allow any occurrence whatever to deprive him of his responsibility for the course of history—because he knows that it has been laid on him by God—will thereafter achieve a more fruitful relation to the events of history than that of barren criticism and equally barren opportunism. To talk of going down fighting like heroes in the face of certain defeat is not really heroic at all, but merely a refusal to face the future. The ultimate question for a responsible man to ask is not how he is to extricate himself heroically from the affair, but how the coming generation is to live. It is only from this question, with its responsibility towards history, that fruitful solutions can come, even if for the time being they are very humiliating. In short, it is much easier to see a thing through from the point of view of abstract principle than from that of concrete responsibility. The rising generation will always instinctively discern which of these we make the basis of our actions, for it is their own future that is at stake.

Of Folly

FOLLY IS A MORE DANGEROUS ENEMY to the good than evil. One can protest against evil; it can be unmasked and, if need be, prevented by force. Evil always carries the seeds of its own destruction, as it makes people, at the least, uncomfortable. Against folly we have no defence. Neither protests nor force can touch it; reasoning is no use; facts that contradict personal prejudices can simply be disbelieved—indeed, the fool can counter by criticizing them, and if they are undeniable, they can just be pushed aside as trivial exceptions. So the fool, as distinct from the scoundrel, is completely self-satisfied; in fact, he can easily become dangerous, as it does not take much to make him aggressive. A fool must therefore be treated more cautiously than a scoundrel; we shall never again try to convince a fool by reason, for it is both useless and dangerous.

If we are to deal adequately with folly, we must try to understand its nature. This much is certain, that it is a moral rather than an intellectual defect. There are people who are mentally agile but foolish, and people who are mentally slow but very far from foolish—a discovery that we make to our surprise as a result of particular situations. We thus get the impression that folly is likely to be, not a congenital defect, but one that is acquired in certain circumstances where people *make* fools of themselves or allow others to make fools of them. We notice further that this defect is less common in the unsociable and solitary than in individuals or groups that are inclined or condemned to sociability. It seems, then, that folly is a sociological rather than a psychological problem, and that it is a special form of the operation of historical circumstances on people, a psychological by-product of definite external factors. If we look more closely, we see that any violent display of power, whether political or religious, produces an outburst of folly in a large part of mankind; indeed, this seems actually to be a psychological and sociological law: the power of some needs the folly of the others. It is not that certain human capacities, intellectual capacities for instance, become stunted or destroyed, but rather that the upsurge of power makes such an overwhelming impression that men are deprived of their independent judgment, and—more or less unconsciously—give up trying to assess the new state of affairs for themselves. The fact that the fool is often stubborn must not mislead us into thinking that he is independent. One feels in fact, when talking to him, that one is dealing, not with the man himself, but with slogans, catchwords, and the like, which have taken hold of him. He is under a spell, he is blinded, his very nature is being misused and exploited. Having thus become a passive instrument, the fool will be capable of any evil and at the same time incapable of seeing that it is evil. Here lies the danger of a diabolical exploitation that can do irreparable damage to human beings.

But at this point it is quite clear, too, that folly can be overcome, not by instruction, but only by an act of liberation; and so we have come to terms with the fact that in the great majority of cases inward liberation must be preceded by outward liberation, and that until that has taken place, we may as well abandon all attempts to convince the fool. In this state of affairs we have to realize why it is no use our trying to find out what 'the people' really think, and why the question is so superfluous for the man who thinks and acts responsibly—but always given these particular circumstances. The Bible's words that 'the fear of the Lord is the beginning of wisdom' (Ps. 111:10) tell us that a person's inward liberation to live a responsible life before God is the only real cure for folly.

But there is some consolation in these thoughts on folly: they in no way justify us in thinking that most people are fools in all circumstances. What will really matter is whether those in power expect more from people's folly than from their wisdom and independence of mind.

Confidence

THERE IS HARDLY ONE OF US who has not known what it is to be betrayed. The figure of Judas, which we used to find so difficult to understand, is now fairly familiar to us. The air that we breathe is so polluted by mistrust that it almost chokes us. But where we have broken through the layer of mistrust, we have been able to discover a confidence hitherto undreamed of. Where we trust, we have learnt to put our very lives into the hands of others; in the face of all the different interpretations that have been put on our lives and actions, we have learnt to trust unreservedly. We now know that only such confidence, which is always a venture, though a glad and positive venture, enables us really to live and work. We know that it is most reprehensible to sow and encourage mistrust, and that our duty is rather to foster and strengthen confidence wherever we can. Trust will always be one of the greatest, rarest, and happiest blessings of our life in community, though it can emerge only on the dark background of a necessary mistrust. We have learnt never to trust a scoundrel an inch, but to give ourselves to the trustworthy without reserve.

Sympathy

WE MUST ALLOW for the fact that most people learn wisdom only by personal experience. This explains, first, why so few people are capable of taking precautions in advance— they always fancy that they will somehow or other avoid the danger, till it is too late. Secondly, it explains their insensibility to the sufferings of others; sympathy grows in proportion to the fear of approaching disaster. There is a good deal of excuse on ethical grounds for this attitude. No one wants to meet fate head-on; inward calling and strength for action are acquired only in the actual emergency. No one is responsible for all the injustice and suffering in the world, and no one wants to set himself up as the judge of the world. Psychologically, our lack of imagination, of sensitivity, and of mental alertness is balanced by a steady composure, an ability to go on working, and a great capacity for suffering. But from a Christian point of view, none of these excuses can obscure the fact that the most important factor, large-heartedness, is lacking. Christ kept himself from suffering till his hour had come, but when it did come he met it as a free man, seized it, and mastered it. Christ, so the scriptures tell us, bore the sufferings of all humanity in his own body as if they were his own—a thought beyond our comprehension—accepting them of his own free will. We are certainly not Christ; we are not called on to redeem the world by our own deeds and sufferings, and we need not try to assume such an impossible burden. We are not lords, but instruments in the hand of the Lord of history; and we can share in other people's sufferings only to a very limited degree. We are not Christ, but if we want to be Christians, we must have some share in Christ's large-heartedness by acting with responsibility and in freedom when the hour of danger comes, and by showing a real sympathy that springs, not from fear, but from the liberating and redeeming love of Christ for all who suffer. Mere waiting and looking on is not Christian behaviour. The Christian is called to sympathy and action, not in the first place by his own sufferings, but by the sufferings of his brethren, for whose sake Christ suffered.

Optimism

IT IS WISER to be pessimistic; it is a way of avoiding disappointment and ridicule, and so wise people condemn optimism. The essence of optimism is not its view of the present, but the fact that it is the inspiration of life and hope when others give in; it enables a man to hold his head high when everything seems to be going wrong; it gives him strength to sustain reverses and yet to claim the future for himself instead of abandoning it to his opponent. It is true that there is a silly, cowardly kind of optimism, which we must condemn. But the optimism that is will for the future should never be despised, even if it is proved wrong a hundred times; it is health and vitality, and the sick man has no business to impugn it.

There are people who regard it as frivolous, and some Christians think it impious for anyone to hope and prepare for a better earthly future. They think that the meaning of present events is chaos, disorder, and catastrophe; and in resignation or pious escapism they surrender all responsibility for reconstruction and for future generations. It may be that the day of judgement will dawn tomorrow; in that case, we shall gladly stop working for a better future. But not before.

Gratefulness

...I THINK we honour God more if we gratefully accept the life that he gives us with all its blessings, loving it and drinking it to the full, and also grieving deeply and sincerely when we have impaired or wasted any of the good things of life (some people denounce such an attitude, and think it is bourgeois, weak, and sensitive), than if we are insensitive to life's blessings and may therefore also be insensitive to pain. Job's words, 'The Lord gave etc. . . .' include rather than exclude this, as can be seen clearly enough from his teeth-clenching speeches which were vindicated by God (42:7ff.) in face of the false, premature, pious submission of his friends. . . .

Deputyship

THE FACT that responsibility is fundamentally a matter of deputyship is demonstrated most clearly in those circumstances in which a man is directly obliged to act in the place of other men, for example as a father, as a statesman or as a teacher. The father acts for the children, working for them, caring for them, interceding, fighting and suffering for them. Thus in a real sense he is their deputy. He is not an isolated individual, but he combines in himself the selves of a number of human beings. Any attempt to live as though he were alone is a denial of the actual fact of his responsibility. He cannot evade the responsibility which is laid on him with his paternity. This reality shatters the fiction that the subject, the performer, of all ethical conduct is the isolated individual. Not the individual in isolation but the responsible man is the subject, the agent, with whom ethical reflexion must concern itself. This principle is not affected by the extent of the responsibility assumed, whether it be for a single human being, for a community or for whole groups of communities. No man can altogether escape responsibility, and this means that no man can avoid deputyship. Even the solitary lives as a deputy, and indeed quite especially so, for his life is lived in deputyship for man as man, for mankind as a whole. And, in fact, the concept of responsibility for oneself possesses a meaning only in so far as it refers to the responsibility which I bear with respect to myself as a man, that is to say, because I am a man. Responsibility for oneself is in truth responsibility with respect to the man, and that means responsibility with respect to mankind. The fact that Jesus lived without the special responsibility of a marriage, of a family or of a profession, does not by any means set Him outside the field of responsibility; on the contrary, it makes all the clearer His responsibility and His deputyship for all men. Here we come already to the underlying basis of everything that has been said so far. Jesus, life, our life, lived in deputyship for us as the incarnate Son of God, and that is why through Him all human life is in essence a life of deputyship. Jesus was not the individual, desiring to achieve a perfection of his own, but He lived only as the one who has taken up into Himself and who bears within Himself the selves of all men. All His living, His action and His dying was deputyship. In Him there is fulfilled what the living, the action and the suffering of men ought to be. In this real deputyship which constitutes His human existence He is the responsible person *par excellence.* Because He is life all life is determined by Him to be deputyship. Whether or not life resists, it is now always deputyship, for life or for death, just as the father is always a father, for good or for evil.

Lust

WHAT DOES THE BIBLE SAY about the lust of men as the author of their temptation? "Let no man say when he is tempted, I am tempted of God: for God cannot be tempted with evil, and he himself tempteth no man: but each man is tempted, when he is drawn away by his own lust, and enticed. Then the lust, when it hath conceived, beareth sin: and the sin, when it is fullgrown, bringeth forth death" (James 1:31ff.).

First, he who transfers the guilt of the temptation to someone other than himself, thereby justifies his fall. If I am not guilty in my temptation, neither am I guilty when I perish in it. Temptation is guilt in so far as the fall is inexcusable. It is therefore impossible to put the guilt of temptation on to the devil; then all the more is it a blasphemy to make God answerable for it. It may appear pious, but in truth the statement implies that God is himself in some way open to evil. This would attribute division to God, which makes his Word and his will questionable, ambiguous, doubtful. Since evil has no place in God, not even the possibility of evil, temptation to evil must never be laid at God's door. God himself tempts no one. The source of temptation lies in my own self. Secondly, temptation is punishment. The place in which all temptation originates is my evil desires. My own longing for pleasure, and my fear of suffering, entice me to let go the Word of God. The hereditary depraved nature of the flesh is the source of the evil inclinations of body and soul, as are men and things, which now become temptation. Neither the beauty of the world, nor suffering, are in themselves evil and tempting, but our evil desires which win pleasure from all this and which let themselves be suborned and enticed, turn all this into temptation for us. While in the devilish origin of temptation the objectivity of temptation must become clear, here its complete subjectivity is emphasized. Both are equally necessary.

Thirdly, desire in itself does not make me sinful. But "when it hath conceived, it beareth sin, and the sin, when it is fullgrown, bringeth forth death." Desire conceives by the union of my "I" with it—when I abandon the Word of God which upholds me. As long as desire remains untouched by my self, it is an "It." But sin occurs only through the "I." Thus the source of temptation lies in the ἐπιθυμία, the source of sin is in myself, and in my self alone. Therefore I must acknowledge that mine alone is the guilt and that I deserve eternal death when in temptation I succumb to sin. Jesus indeed pronounces a terrible judgement on him who tempts the innocent, who offends one of the little ones; "Woe unto him who tempts another to sin"—that is what the Word of God says about every tempter. But yours alone is the guilt in your sin and your death, if you submit to the temptation of your desire. That is God's Word to the tempted.

Shame

INSTEAD OF SEEING GOD man sees himself. 'Their eyes were opened' (Gen. 3:7). Man perceives himself in his disunion with God and with men. He perceives that he is naked. Lacking the protection, the covering, which God and his fellow-man afforded him, he finds himself laid bare. Hence there arises shame. Shame is man's ineffaceable recollection of his estrangement from the origin; it is grief for this estrangement, and the powerless longing to return to unity with the origin. Man is ashamed because he has lost something which is essential to his original character, to himself as a whole; he is ashamed of his nakedness. Just as in the fairy-story the tree is ashamed of its lack of adornment, so, too, man is ashamed of the loss of his unity with God and with other men. Shame and remorse are generally mistaken for one another. Man feels remorse when he has been at fault; and he feels shame because he lacks something. Shame is more original than remorse. The peculiar fact that we lower our eyes when a stranger's eye meets our gaze is not a sign of remorse for a fault, but a sign of that shame which, when it knows that it is seen, is reminded of something that it lacks, namely, the lost wholeness of life, its own nakedness. To meet a stranger's gaze directly, as is required, for example, in making a declaration of personal loyalty, is a kind of act of violence, and in love, when the gaze of the other is sought, it is a kind of yearning. In both cases it is the painful endeavour to recover the lost unity by either a conscious and resolute or else a passionate and devoted inward overcoming of shame as the sign of disunion.[1]

[1] 'Shame isn't spontaneous... it's artificial, it's acquired. You can make people ashamed of anything. Agonizingly ashamed of wearing brown boots with a black coat, or speaking with the wrong sort of accent.... The Christians invented it, just as the tailors in Savile Row invented the shame of wearing brown boots with a black coat' (Aldous Huxley, *Point Counter Point*, chapter x). To this it must be replied that first, embarrassment and diffidence are not to be confused with shame, and, secondly, shame may also find expression in quite external matters in a way which will depend on the character of the individual. The point is that shame may arise wherever there is experience of man's disunion—so why not also in connexion with dress?

Desire

IN OUR MEMBERS there is a slumbering inclination towards desire which is both sudden and fierce. With irresistible power desire seizes mastery over the flesh. All at once a secret, smouldering fire is kindled. The flesh burns and is in flames. It makes no difference whether it is sexual desire, or ambition, or vanity, or desire for revenge, or love of fame and power, or greed for money, or, finally, that strange desire for the beauty of the world, of nature. Joy in God is in course of being extinguished in us and we seek all our joy in the creature. At this moment God is quite unreal to us, he loses all reality, and only desire for the creature is real; the only reality is the devil. Satan does not here fill us with hatred of God, but with forgetfulness of God. And now his falsehood is added to this proof of strength. The lust thus aroused envelops the mind and will of man in deepest darkness. The powers of clear discrimination and of decision are taken from us. The questions present themselves: "Is what the flesh desires really sin in this case?" "Is it really not permitted to me, yes—expected of me, now, here, in my particular situation, to appease desire?" The tempter puts me in a privileged position as he tried to put the hungry Son of God in a privileged position. I boast of my privilege against God.

It is here that everything within me rises up against the Word of God. Powers of the body, the mind and the will, which were held in obedience under the discipline of the Word, of which I believed that I was the master, make it clear to me that I am by no means master of them. "All my powers forsake me," laments the psalmist. They have all gone over to the adversary. The adversary deploys my powers against me. In this situation I can no longer act as a hero; I am a defenceless, powerless man. God himself has forsaken me. Who can conquer, who can gain the victory?

None other than the Crucified, Jesus Christ himself, for whose sake all this happens to me; for he is by me and in me, and therefore temptation besets me as it beset him.

Conscience

JESUS CHRIST has become my conscience. This means that I can now find unity with myself only in the surrender of my ego to God and to men. The origin and the goal of my conscience is not a law but it is the living God and the living man as he confronts me in Jesus Christ. For the sake of God and of men Jesus became a breaker of the law. He broke the law of the Sabbath in order to keep it holy in love for God and for men. He forsook His parents in order to dwell in the house of His Father and thereby to purify His obedience towards His parents. He sat at table with sinners and outcasts; and for the love of men He came to be forsaken by God in His last hour. As the one who loved without sin, He became guilty; He wished to share in the fellowship of human guilt; He rejected the devil's accusation which was intended to divert Him from this course. Thus it is Jesus Christ who sets conscience free for the service of God and of our neighbour; He sets conscience free even and especially when man enters into the fellowship of human guilt. The conscience which has been set free from the law will not be afraid to enter into the guilt of another man for the other man's sake, and indeed precisely in doing this it will show itself in its purity. The conscience which has been set free is not timid like the conscience which is bound by the law, but it stands wide open for our neighbour and for his concrete distress. And so conscience joins with the responsibility which has its foundation in Christ in bearing guilt for the sake of our neighbour. Human action is poisoned in a way which differs from essential original sin, yet as responsible action, in contrast to any self-righteously high-principled action, it nevertheless indirectly has a part in the action of Jesus Christ. For responsible action, therefore, there is a kind of relative freedom from sin, and this shows itself precisely in the responsible acceptance of the guilt of others.

Humanity and Goodness

...Whatever humanity and goodness is found in this fallen world must be on the side of Jesus Christ. It is nothing less than a curtailment of the gospel if the nearness of Jesus Christ is proclaimed only to what is broken and evil and if the father's love for the prodigal son is so emphasized as to appear to diminish his love for the son who remained at home. Certainly the humanity and goodness of which we are speaking are not the humanity and goodness of Jesus Christ; they cannot stand before the judgement; and yet Jesus loved the young man who had kept the commandments (Mark 10:17ff.). Humanity and goodness should not acquire a value on their own account, but they should and shall be claimed for Jesus Christ, especially in cases where they persist as the unconscious residue of a former attachment to the ultimate. It may often seem more in earnest to treat a man in this situation simply as a non-Christian and to urge him to confess his unbelief. But it will be more Christian to claim precisely that man as a Christian who would himself no longer dare to call himself a Christian, and then with much patience to help him to the profession of faith in Christ.

The Pharisee

IT IS IN JESUS' MEETING with the Pharisee that the old and the new are most clearly contrasted. The correct understanding of this meeting is of the greatest significance for the understanding of the gospel as a whole. The Pharisee is not an adventitious historical phenomenon of a particular time. He is the man to whom only the knowledge of good and evil has come to be of importance in his entire life; in other words, he is simply the man of disunion. Any distorted picture of the Pharisees robs Jesus' argument with them of its gravity and its importance. The Pharisee is that extremely admirable man who subordinates his entire life to his knowledge of good and evil and is as severe a judge of himself as of his neighbour to the honour of God, whom he humbly thanks for this knowledge. For the Pharisee every moment of life becomes a situation of conflict in which he has to choose between good and evil. For the sake of avoiding any lapse his entire thought is strenuously devoted night and day to the anticipation of the whole immense range of possible conflicts, to the reaching of a decision in these conflicts, and to the determination of his own choice. There are innumerable factors to be observed, guarded against and distinguished. The finer the distinctions the surer will be the correct decision. This observation extends to the whole of life in all its manifold aspects. The Pharisee is not opinionated; special situations and emergencies receive special considerations; forbearance and generosity are not excluded by the gravity of the knowledge of good and evil; they are rather an expression of this gravity. And there is no rash presumption here, or arrogance or unverified self-esteem. The Pharisee is fully conscious of his own faults and of his duty of humility and thankfulness towards God. But, of course, there are differences, which for God's sake must not be disregarded, between the sinner and the man who strives towards good, between the man who becomes a breaker of the law out of a situation of wickedness and the man who does so out of necessity. If anyone disregards these differences, if he fails to take every factor into account in each of the innumerable cases of conflict, he sins against the knowledge of good and evil.

Judgement

'JUDGE NOT, that ye be not judged' (Matt. 7:1). This is not an exhortation to prudence and forbearance in passing judgement on one's fellow-men, such as was also recognized by the Pharisees. It is a blow struck at the heart of the man who knows good and evil. It is the word of Him who speaks by virtue of his unity with God, who came not to condemn but to save (John 3:17). For man in the state of disunion good consists in passing judgement, and the ultimate criterion is man himself. Knowing good and evil, man is essentially a judge. As a judge he is like God, except that every judgement he delivers falls back upon himself. In attacking man as a judge Jesus is demanding the conversion of his entire being, and He shows that precisely in the extreme realization of his good he is ungodly and a sinner. Jesus demands that the knowledge of good and evil be overcome; He demands unity with God. Judgement passed on another man always presupposes disunion with him; it is an obstacle to action. But the good of which Jesus speaks consists entirely in action and not in judgement. Judging the other man always means a break in one's own activity. The man who judges never acts himself; or, alternatively, whatever action of his own he may be able to show, and sometimes indeed there is plenty of it, is never more than judgement, condemnation, reproaches and accusations against other men. . . .

Single-minded Love

WHEN WE JUDGE other people we confront them in a spirit of detachment, observing and reflecting as it were from the outside. But love has neither time nor opportunity for this. If we love, we can never observe the other person with detachment, for he is always and at every moment a living claim to our love and service. But does not the evil in the other person make me condemn him just for his own good, for the sake of love? Here we see the depth of the dividing line. Any misguided love for the sinner is ominously close to the love of sin. But the love of Christ for the sinner in itself is the condemnation of sin, is his expression of extreme hatred of sin. The disciples of Christ are to love unconditionally. Thus they may effect what their own divided and judiciously and conditionally offered love never could achieve, namely the radical condemnation of sin.

If the disciples make judgements of their own, they set up standards of good and evil. But Jesus Christ is not a standard which I can apply to others. He is judge of myself, revealing my own virtues to me as something altogether evil. Thus I am not permitted to apply to the other person what does not apply to me. For, with my judgement according to good and evil, I only affirm the other person's evil, for he does exactly the same. But he does not know of the hidden iniquity of the good but seeks his justification in it. If I condemn his evil actions I thereby confirm him in his apparently good actions which are yet never the good commended by Christ. Thus we remove him from the judgement of Christ and subject him to human judgement. But I bring God's judgement upon my head, for I then do not live any more on and out of the grace of Jesus Christ, but out of my knowledge of good and evil which I hold on to. To everyone God is the kind of God he believes in.

Judgement is the forbidden objectivization of the other person which destroys single-minded love. I am not forbidden to have my own thoughts about the other person, to realize his shortcomings, but only to the extent that it offers to me an occasion for forgiveness and unconditional love, as Jesus proves to me. If I withhold my judgement I am not indulging in *tout comprendre c'est tout pardonner* and confirm the other person in his bad ways. Neither I am right nor the other person, but God is always right and shall proclaim both his grace and his judgement. . . .

The Concept of Reality

WHOEVER WISHES to take up the problem of a Christian ethic must be confronted at once with a demand which is quite without parallel. He must from the outset discard as irrelevant the two questions which alone impel him to concern himself with the problem of ethics, 'How can I be good?' and 'How can I do good?', and instead of these he must ask the utterly and totally different question 'What is the will of God?' This requirement is so immensely far-reaching because it presupposes a decision with regard to the ultimate reality; it presupposes a decision of faith. If the ethical problem presents itself essentially in the form of enquiries about one's own being good and doing good, this means that it has already been decided that it is the self and the world which are the ultimate reality. The aim of all ethical reflection is, then, that I myself shall be good and that the world shall become good through my action. But the problem of ethics at once assumes a new aspect if it becomes apparent that these realities, myself and the world, themselves lie embedded in a quite different ultimate reality, namely, the reality of God, the Creator, Reconciler and Redeemer. What is of ultimate importance is now no longer that I should become good, or that the condition of the world should be made better by my action, but that the reality of God should show itself everywhere to be the ultimate reality. Where there is faith in God as the ultimate reality, all concern with ethics will have as its starting-point that God shows Himself to be good, even if this involves the risk that I myself and the world are not good but thoroughly bad. All things appear distorted if they are not seen and recognized in God. All so-called data, all laws and standards, are mere abstractions so long as there is no belief in God as the ultimate reality. But when we say that God is the ultimate reality, this is not an idea, through which the world as we have it is to be sublimated. It is not the religious rounding-off of a profane conception of the universe. It is the acceptance in faith of God's showing forth of Himself, the acceptance of His revelation. If God were merely a religious idea there would be nothing to prevent us from discerning, behind this allegedly 'ultimate' reality, a still more final reality, the twilight of the gods and the death of the gods. The claim of this ultimate reality is satisfied only in so far as it is revelation, that is to say, the self-witness of the living God. When this is so, the relation to this reality determines the whole of life. The apprehension of this reality is not merely a gradual advance towards the discovery of ever more profound realities; it is the crucial turning-point in the apprehension of reality as a whole. The ultimate reality now shows itself to be at the same time the initial reality, the first and last, alpha and omega. Any perception or apprehension of things or laws without Him is now abstraction, detachment from the origin and goal. Any enquiry about one's own goodness, or the goodness of the world, is now impossible unless enquiry has first been made about the goodness of God. For without God what meaning could there be in a goodness of man and a goodness of the world? But God as the ultimate reality is no other than He who shows forth, manifests and reveals Himself, that is to say, God in Jesus Christ, and from this it follows that the question of good can find its answer only in Christ.

Divine Reality

THE PROBLEM of Christian ethics is the realization among God's creatures of the revelational reality of God in Christ, just as the problem of dogmatics is the truth of the revelational reality of God in Christ. The place which in all other ethics is occupied by the antithesis of 'should be' and 'is', idea and accomplishment, motive and performance, is occupied in Christian ethics by the relation of reality and realization, past and present, history and event (faith), or, to replace the equivocal concept by the unambiguous name, the relation of Jesus Christ and the

Holy Spirit. The question of good becomes the question of participation in the divine reality which is revealed in Christ. Good is now no longer a valuation of what is, a valuation, for example, of my own being, my outlook or my actions, or of some condition or state in the world. It is no longer a predicate that is assigned to something which is in itself in being. Good is the real itself. It is not the real in the abstract, the real which is detached from the reality of God, but the real which possesses reality only in God. There is no good without the real, for the good is not a general formula, and the real is impossible without the good. The wish to be good consists solely in the longing for what is real in God. A desire to be good for its own sake, as an end in itself, so to speak, or as a vocation in life, falls victim to the irony of unreality. The genuine striving for good now becomes the self-assertiveness of the prig. Good is not in itself an independent theme for life; if it were so it would be the craziest kind of quixotry. Only if we share in reality can we share in good.

The Reality of God

...CHRISTIAN BELIEF deduces that the reality of God is not in itself merely an idea from the fact that this reality of God has manifested and revealed itself in the midst of the real world. In Jesus Christ the reality of God entered into the reality of this world. The place where the answer is given, both to the question concerning the reality of God and to the question concerning the reality of the world, is designated solely and alone by the name Jesus Christ. God and the world are comprised in this name. In Him all things consist (Col. 1:17). Henceforward one can speak neither of God nor of the world without speaking of Jesus Christ. All concepts of reality which do not take account of Him are abstractions. When good has become reality in Jesus Christ, there is no more force in any discussion of good which plays off what should be against what is and what is against what should be. Jesus Christ cannot be identified either with an ideal or standard or with things as they are. The hostility of the ideal towards things as they are, the fanatical putting into effect of an idea in the face of a resisting actuality, may be as remote from good as is the sacrifice of what should be to what is expedient. Both what should be and what is expedient acquire in Christ an entirely new meaning. The irreconcilable conflict between what is and what should be is reconciled in Christ, that is to say, in the ultimate reality. Participation in this reality is the true sense and purpose of the enquiry concerning good.

In Christ we are offered the possibility of partaking in the reality of God and in the reality of the world, but not in the one without the other. The reality of God discloses itself only by setting me entirely in the reality of the world, and when I encounter the reality of the world it is always already sustained, accepted and reconciled in the reality of God. This is the inner meaning of the revelation of God in the man Jesus Christ. Christian ethics enquires about the realization in our world of this divine and cosmic reality which is given in Christ. This does not mean that 'our world' is something outside the divine and cosmic reality which is in Christ, or that it is not already part of the world which is sustained, accepted and reconciled in Him. It does not mean that one must still begin by applying some kind of 'principle' to our situation and our time. The enquiry is directed rather towards the way in which the reality in Christ, which for a long time already has comprised us and our world within itself, is taking effect as something now present, and towards the way in which life may be conducted in this reality. Its purpose is, therefore, participation in the reality of God and of the world in Jesus Christ today, and this participation must be such that I never experience the reality of God without the reality of the world or the reality of the world without the reality of God.

The Reality of Jesus Christ

...THERE IS NO PLACE to which the Christian can withdraw from the world, whether it be outwardly or in the sphere of the inner life. Any attempt to escape from the world must sooner or later be paid for with a sinful surrender to the world. It is after all a matter of experience that when the gross sins of sex have been overcome they are succeeded by covetousness and avarice, which are equally gross sins even though the world may treat them less severely. The cultivation of a Christian inner life, untouched by the world, will generally present a somewhat tragicomical appearance to the worldly observer. For the sharp-sighted world recognizes itself most distinctly at the very point where the Christian inner life deceives itself in the belief that the world is most remote. Whoever professes to believe in the reality of Jesus Christ, as the revelation of God, must in the same breath profess his faith in both the reality of God and the reality of the world; for in Christ he finds God and the world reconciled. And for just this reason the Christian is no longer the man of eternal conflict, but, just as the reality in Christ is one, so he, too, since he shares in this reality in Christ, is himself an undivided whole. His worldliness does not divide him from Christ and his Christianity does not divide him from the world. Belonging wholly to Christ, he stands at the same time wholly in the world.

Christ, Reality and Good

CHRIST AND HIS ADVERSARY, the devil, are mutually exclusive contraries; yet the devil must serve Christ even against his will; he desires evil, but over and over again he is compelled to do good; so that the realm or space of the devil is always only beneath the feet of Jesus Christ. But if the kingdom of the devil is taken to mean that world which 'lies in disorder', the world which has fallen under the devil's authority, then here, especially, there is a limit to the possibility of thinking in terms of spheres. For it is precisely this 'disordered' world that in Christ is reconciled with God and that now possesses its final and true reality not in the devil but in Christ. The world is not divided between Christ and the devil, but, whether it recognizes it or not, it is solely and entirely the world of Christ. The world is to be called to this, its reality in Christ, and in this way the false reality will be destroyed which it believes that it possesses in itself as in the devil. The dark and evil world must not be abandoned to the devil. It must be claimed for Him who has won it by His incarnation, His death and His resurrection. Christ gives up nothing of what He has won. He holds it fast in His hands. It is Christ, therefore, who renders inadmissible the dichotomy of a bedevilled and a Christian world. Any static delimitation of a region which belongs to the devil and a region which belongs to Christ is a denial of the reality of God's having reconciled the whole world with Himself in Christ.

That God loved the world and reconciled it with Himself in Christ is the central message proclaimed in the New Testament. It is assumed there that the world stands in need of reconciliation with God but that it is not capable of achieving it by itself. The acceptance of the world by God is a miracle of the divine compassion. For this reason the relation of the Church to the world is determined entirely by the relation of God to the world. There is a love for the world which is enmity towards God (Jas. 4:4) because it springs from the nature of the world as such and not from the love of God for the world. The world 'as such' is the world as it understands itself, the world which resists and even rejects the reality of the love of God which is bestowed upon it in Jesus Christ. This world has fallen under the sentence which God passes on all enmity to Christ. It is engaged in a life-and-death struggle with the Church. And yet it is the task and the essential character of the Church that she shall impart to precisely this world its reconciliation with God and that she shall open its eyes to the reality of the love of God, against which it is blindly raging. In this way it is also, and indeed especially, the lost and sentenced world that is incessantly drawn in into the event of Christ.

What Is Meant By 'Telling the Truth'?

FROM THE MOMENT IN OUR LIVES at which we learn to speak we are taught that what we say must be true. What does

Editor's note: Written after intensive interrogation.

this mean? What is meant by 'telling the truth'? What does it demand of us?

It is clear that in the first place it is our parents who regulate our relation to themselves by this demand for truthfulness; consequently, in the sense in which our parents intend it, this demand applies strictly only within the family circle. It is also to be noted that the relation which is expressed in this demand cannot simply be reversed. The truthfulness of a child towards his parents is essentially different from that of the parents towards their child. The life of the small child lies open before the parents, and what the child says should reveal to them everything that is hidden and secret, but in the converse relationship this cannot possibly be the case. Consequently, in the matter of truthfulness, the parents' claim on the child is different from the child's claim on the parents.

From this it emerges already that 'telling the truth' means something different according to the particular situation in which one stands. Account must be taken of one's relationships at each particular time. The question must be asked whether and in what way a man is entitled to demand truthful speech of others. Speech between parents and children is, in the nature of the case, different from speech between man and wife, between friends, between teacher and pupil, government and subject, friend and foe, and in each case the truth which this speech conveys is also different.

It will at once be objected that one does not owe truthful speech to this or that individual man, but solely to God. This objection is correct so long as it is not forgotten that God is not a general principle, but the living God who has set me in a living life and who demands service of me within this living life. If one speaks of God one must not simply disregard the actual given world in which one lives; for if one does that one is not speaking of the God who entered into the world in Jesus Christ, but rather of some metaphysical idol. And it is precisely this which is determined by the way in which, in my actual concrete life with all its manifold relationships, I give effect to the truthfulness which I owe to God. The truthfulness which we owe to God must assume a concrete form in the world. Our speech must be truthful, not in principle but concretely. A truthfulness which is not concrete is not truthful before God.

Satanic Truth

THERE IS A TRUTH which is of Satan. Its essence is that under the semblance of truth it denies everything that is real. It lives upon hatred of the real and of the world which is created and loved by God. It pretends to be executing the judgement of God upon the fall of the real. God's truth judges created things out of love, and Satan's truth judges them out of envy and hatred. God's truth has become flesh in the world and is alive in the real, but Satan's truth is the death of all reality.

Who Am I?

WHO AM I? They often tell me
I would step from my cell's confinement
calmly, cheerfully, firmly,
like a squire from his country-house.

Who am I? They often tell me
I would talk to my warders
freely and friendly and clearly,
as though it were mine to command.

Who am I? They also tell me
I would bear the days of misfortune
equably, smilingly, proudly,
like one accustomed to win.

Am I then really all that which other men tell of?
Or am I only what I know of myself,
restless and longing and sick, like a bird in a cage,
struggling for breath, as though hands were compres-
        sing my throat,
yearning for colours, for flowers, for the voices of
        birds,
thirsting for words of kindness, for neighbourliness,
trembling with anger at despotisms and petty
        humiliation,
tossing in expectation of great events,
powerlessly trembling for friends at an infinite
        distance,

weary and empty at praying, at thinking, at making,
faint, and ready to say farewell to it all?

Who am I? This or the other?
Am I one person today, and tomorrow another?
Am I both at once? A hypocrite before others,
and before myself a contemptibly woebegone
 weakling?
Or is something within me still like a beaten army,
fleeing in disorder from victory already achieved?

Who am I? They mock me, these lonely questions of
 mine.
Whoever I am, thou knowest, O God, I am thine.

Our Lives

...I THINK it is a literal fact of nature that human life
extends far beyond our physical existence. Probably a
mother feels this more strongly than anyone else. There
are two passages in the Bible which always seem to me to
sum the thing up. One is from Jeremiah 45: 'Behold, what
I have built I am breaking down, and what I have planted I
am plucking up...And do you seek great things for
yourself? Seek them not...but I will give your life as a
prize of war...'; and the other is from Psalm 60: 'Thou
hast made the land to quake, thou hast rent it open; repair
its breaches, for it totters.'

Freedom from Anxiety

(MATTHEW 6:25–34)

BE NOT ANXIOUS! Earthly possessions dazzle our eyes and delude us into thinking that they can provide security and freedom from anxiety. Yet all the time they are the very source of all anxiety. If our hearts are set on them, our reward is an anxiety whose burden is intolerable. Anxiety creates its own treasures and they in turn beget further care. When we seek for security in possessions we are trying to drive out care with care, and the net result is the precise opposite of our anticipations. The fetters which bind us to our possessions prove to be cares themselves.

The way to misuse our possessions is to use them as an insurance against the morrow. Anxiety is always directed to the morrow, whereas goods are in the strictest sense meant to be used only for to-day. By trying to ensure for the next day we are only creating uncertainty to-day. Sufficient unto the day is the evil thereof. The only way to win assurance is by leaving to-morrow entirely in the hands of God and by receiving from him all we need for to-day. If instead of receiving God's gifts for to-day we worry about to-morrow, we find ourselves helpless victims of infinite anxiety. "Be not anxious for the morrow": either that is cruel mockery for the poor and wretched, the very people Jesus is talking to who, humanly speaking, really will starve if they do not make provision to-day. Either it is an intolerable law, which men will reject with indignation; or it is the unique proclamation of the gospel of the glorious liberty of the children of God, who have a Father in heaven, a Father who has given his beloved Son. How shall not God with him also freely give us all things?

"Be not anxious for the morrow." This is not to be taken as a philosophy of life or a moral law: it is the gospel of Jesus Christ, and only so can it be understood. Only those who follow him and know him can receive this word as a promise of the love of his Father and as a deliverance from the thraldom of material things. It is not care that frees the disciples from care, but their faith in Jesus Christ. Only they know that we *cannot* be anxious (verse 27). The coming day, even the coming hour, are placed beyond our control. It is senseless to pretend that we can make provision because we cannot alter the circumstances of this world. Only God can take care, for it is he who rules the world. Since we *cannot* take care, since we are so completely powerless, we *ought* not to do it either. If we do, we are dethroning God and presuming to rule the world ourselves.

But the Christian also knows that he not only cannot and dare not be anxious, but that there is also no need for him to be so. Neither anxiety nor work can secure his daily bread, for bread is the gift of the Father. The birds and lilies neither toil nor spin, yet both are fed and clothed and receive their daily portion without being anxious for them. They need earthly goods only for their daily sustenance, and they do not lay up a store for the future. This is the way they glorify their Creator, not by their industry, toil or care, but by a daily unquestioning acceptance of his gifts. Birds and lilies then are an example for the followers of Christ. "Man-in-revolt" imagines that there is a relation of cause and effect between work and sustenance, but Jesus explodes that illusion. According to him, bread is not to be valued as the reward for work; he speaks instead of the carefree simplicity of the man who walks with him and accepts everything as it comes from God.

. . . Worldly cares are not a part of our discipleship, but distinct and subordinate concerns. Before we start taking thought for our life, our food and clothing, our work and families, we must seek the righteousness of Christ. This is no more than an ultimate summing up of all that has been said before. Again we have here either a crushing burden, which holds out no hope for the poor and wretched, or else it is the quintessence of the gospel, which brings the promise of freedom and perfect joy. Jesus does not tell us what we ought to do but cannot; he tells us what God has given us and promises still to give. If Christ has been given us, if we are called to his discipleship we are given all things, literally *all* things. He will see to it that they are added unto us. If we follow Jesus and look only to his righteousness, we are in his hands and under the protection of him and his Father. And if we are in communion with the Father, nought can harm us. We shall always be assured that he can feed his children and will not suffer them to hunger. God will help us in the hour of need, and he knows our needs.

After he has been following Christ for a long time, the disciple of Jesus will be asked "Lacked ye anything?" and he will answer "Nothing, Lord." How could he when he knows that despite hunger and nakedness, persecution and danger, the Lord is always at his side?

Are We Still of Any Use?

WE HAVE BEEN SILENT witnesses of evil deeds; we have been drenched by many storms; we have learnt the arts of equivocation and pretence; experience has made us suspicious of others and kept us from being truthful and open; intolerable conflicts have worn us down and even made us cynical. Are we still of any use? What we shall need is not geniuses, or cynics, or misanthropes, or clever tacticians, but plain, honest, straightforward men. Will our inward power of resistance be strong enough, and our honesty with ourselves remorseless enough, for us to find our way back to simplicity and straightforwardness?

Who Stands Fast?

THE GREAT MASQUERADE of evil has played havoc with all our ethical concepts. For evil to appear disguised as light, charity, historical necessity, or social justice is quite bewildering to anyone brought up on our traditional ethical concepts, while for the Christian who bases his life on the Bible it merely confirms the fundamental wickedness of evil.

The *'reasonable'* people's failure is obvious. With the best intentions and a naïve lack of realism, they think that with a little reason they can bend back into position the framework that has got out of joint. In their lack of vision they want to do justice to all sides, and so the conflicting forces wear them down with nothing achieved. Disappointed by the world's unreasonableness, they see themselves condemned to ineffectiveness; they step aside in resignation or collapse before the stronger party.

Still more pathetic is the total collapse of moral *fanaticism*. The fanatic thinks that his single-minded principles qualify him to do battle with the powers of evil; but like a bull he rushes at the red cloak instead of the person who is holding it; he exhausts himself and is beaten. He gets entangled in non-essentials and falls into the trap set by cleverer people.

Then there is the man with a *conscience*, who fights single-handed against heavy odds in situations that call for a decision. But the scale of the conflicts in which he has to choose—with no advice or support except from his own conscience—tears him to pieces. Evil approaches him in so many respectable and seductive disguises that his conscience becomes nervous and vacillating, till at last he contents himself with a salved instead of a clear conscience, so that he lies to his own conscience in order to avoid despair; for a man whose only support is his conscience can never realize that a bad conscience may be stronger and more wholesome than a deluded one.

From the perplexingly large number of possible decisions, the way of *duty* seems to be the sure way out. Here, what is commanded is accepted as what is most certain, and the responsibility for it rests on the commander, not on the person commanded. But no one who confines himself to the limits of duty ever goes so far as to venture, on his sole responsibility, to act in the only way that makes it possible to score a direct hit on evil and defeat it. The man of duty will in the end have to do his duty by the devil too.

As to the man who asserts his complete *freedom* to stand four-square to the world, who values the necessary deed more highly than an unspoilt conscience or reputation, who is ready to sacrifice a barren principle for a fruitful compromise, or the barren wisdom of a middle course for a fruitful radicalism—let him beware lest his freedom should bring him down. He will assent to what is bad so as to ward off something worse, and in doing so he will no longer be able to realize that the worse, which he wants to avoid, might be the better. Here we have the raw material of tragedy.

Here and there people flee from public altercation into the sanctuary of private *virtuousness*. But anyone who does this must shut his mouth and his eyes to the injustice around him. Only at the cost of self-deception can he keep himself pure from the contamination arising from responsible action. In spite of all that he does, what he leaves undone will rob him of his peace of mind. He will either go to pieces because of this disquiet, or become the most hypocritical of Pharisees.

Who stands fast? Only the man whose final standard is not his reason, his principles, his conscience, his freedom, or his virtue, but who is ready to sacrifice all this when he is called to obedient and responsible action in faith and in exclusive allegiance to God—the responsible man, who tries to make his whole life an answer to the question and call of God. Where are these responsible people?

The Taking Over
of the Temptations

By the temptation of Jesus Christ the temptation of Adam is brought to an end. As in Adam's temptation all flesh fell, so in the temptation of Jesus Christ all flesh has been snatched away from the power of Satan. For Jesus Christ wore our flesh, he suffered our temptation, and he won the victory from it. Thus today we all wear the flesh which in Jesus Christ vanquished Satan. Both our flesh and we have conquered in the temptation of Jesus. Because Christ was tempted and overcame, we can pray: Lead us not into temptation. For the temptation has already come and been conquered. He did it in our stead. "Look on the temptation of thy Son Jesus Christ and lead *us* not into temptation." Of the granting of that prayer we may and should be certain; we should utter our amen to it, for it *is* granted in Jesus Christ himself. From henceforth *we* shall no longer be led into temptation, but every temptation which happens now is the temptation of Jesus Christ in his members, in his congregation. We are not tempted, *Jesus Christ is tempted in us.*

Because Satan could not bring about the fall of the Son of God, he pursues him now with all temptations in his members. But these last temptations are only the offshoots of the temptation of Jesus on earth; for the power of temptation is broken in the temptation of Jesus. His disciples are to let themselves be found in this temptation, and then the kingdom is assured to them. It is the fundamental word of Jesus to all his disciples. "But ye are they which have continued with me in my temptations, and I appoint unto you a kingdom" (Luke 22:28f.). It is not the temptations of the *disciples* which here receive the promise, but their participation in the life and the temptation of Jesus. The temptations of the disciples fall on *Jesus,* and the temptations of Jesus come upon the disciples. But to share in the atonement of Christ means to share also in Christ's overcoming and victory. It does not mean that the temptations of Christ had finished and that the disciples would no longer suffer them. They will indeed suffer temptations, but it will be the temptations of Jesus Christ which befall them. Christ has also won the victory over these temptations.

It is by the disciples sharing in the temptation of Jesus Christ that Jesus will protect his disciples from other temptation: "Watch and pray, that ye enter not into temptation" (Matt. 26:41). What temptation threatened the disciples in the hour of Gethsemane, if it was not that they should be offended at the passion of Christ, and they would not share in his temptations? So Jesus uses here the petition of the Lord's Prayer: "Lead us not into temptation." Finally, it is the same thing when it says in Hebrews 2:18: "For in that he himself hath suffered being tempted, he is able to succour them that are tempted." This is not only a question of the help which he alone can give who has learnt to know the need and suffering of the other man in his own experience. The true meaning is rather that in my temptations my real succour is only in his temptation; to share in his temptation is the only help in my temptation. Thus I ought not to think of my temptation other than as the temptation of Jesus Christ. In his temptation is my succour; for here only is victory and overcoming.

The practical task of the Christian must, therefore, be to understand all the temptations which come upon him as temptations of Jesus Christ in him, and thus he will be aided. But how does it happen? Before we can speak of the concrete temptations of Christians and their overcoming, the question of the author of the temptation of Christians must be put. Only when the Christian knows with whom he has to do in temptation, can he act rightly in the actual event.

Concrete Temptations and Their Conquest

IN THE CONCRETE TEMPTATION of Christ there is also, therefore, to be distinguished the hand of the devil and the hand of God, there is the question of resistance and of submission in the right place; that is, resistance to the devil is only possible in the fullest submission to the hand of God.

This must now be made clear in detail. Since all temptations of believers are temptations of Christ in his members, of the body of Christ, we speak of these temptations in the analogy of the temptation of Christ. (1)

Of fleshly temptation. (2) Of high spiritual temptation. (3) Of the last temptation. But I Cor. 10:12ff. is true of all temptations: "Wherefore let him that thinketh he standeth take heed lest he fall. There hath no temptation taken you but such as man can bear: but God is faithful, who will not suffer you to be tempted above that ye are able; but will with the temptation make also the way of escape, that ye may be able to endure it." Here St. Paul opposes first all false security and, secondly, all false despondency in face of temptation. No one can be sure even for a moment that he can remain free from temptation. There is no temptation which could not attack me suddenly at this moment. No one can think that Satan is far from him. "Be sober, be watchful: your adversary the devil, as a roaring lion, walketh about, seeking whom he may devour." (I Pet. 5:8). Not for one moment in this life are we secure from temptation and fall. Therefore do not be proud if you see another stumble and fall. Such security will be a snare for you. "Be not high-minded, but fear" (Rom. 11:20). Rather be at all time ready that the tempter find no power in you.

"Watch and pray, that ye enter not into temptation" (Matt. 26:41). Be on your guard against the crafty enemy, pray to God that he hold us fast in his Word and his grace—that is the attitude of the Christian towards temptation.

But the Christian must not be afraid of temptation. If it comes upon him in spite of watching and praying, then he should know that he can conquer every temptation. There is no temptation which cannot be conquered. God knows our abilities, and he will not let us be tempted beyond our power. It is *human* temptation which harasses us, that is to say, it is not too big for us men. God allots to every man that portion which he can bear. That is certain. He who loses courage because of the suddenness and the awfulness of temptation, has forgotten the main point, namely that he will quite certainly withstand the temptation because God will not let it go beyond that which he is able to endure. There are temptations by which we are particularly frightened because we are so often wrecked upon them. When they are suddenly there again, we so often give ourselves up for lost from the beginning. But we must look at these temptations in the greatest peace and composure for they can be conquered, and they are conquered, so certain is it that God is faithful. Temptation must find us in humility and in certainty of victory.

The Legitimate Struggle

ALL TEMPTATION is temptation of Jesus Christ and all victory is victory of Jesus Christ. All temptation leads the believer into the deepest solitude, into abandonment by men and by God. But in this solitude he finds Jesus Christ, man and God. The blood of Christ and the example of Christ and the prayer of Christ are his help and his strength. The Book of Revelation says of the redeemed: "They overcome...because of the blood of the lamb" (Rev. 12:11). Not by the spirit, but by the blood of Christ is the devil overcome. Therefore in all temptation we must get back to this blood, in which is all our help. Then, too, there is the image of Jesus Christ which we should look upon in the hour of temptation. "See the end of the Lord" (James 5:11). His patience in suffering is the death of the flesh, the suffering of our flesh is made to seem of small account, we are preserved from all pride and comforted in all sorrow. The prayer of Jesus Christ which he promised to Peter: "Simon, behold, Satan asked to have you, that he might sift you as wheat, but I made supplication for thee" (Luke 22:31) represents our weak prayer before the Father in heaven, who does not allow us to be tempted beyond our powers.

Believers suffer the hour of temptation without defence. Jesus Christ is their shield. And only when it is quite clearly understood that temptation must befall the Godforsaken, then the word can at last be uttered which the Bible speaks about the Christian's struggle. From heaven the Lord gives to the defenceless the heavenly armour before which, though men's eyes do not see it, Satan flees. *He* clothes us with the armour of God, *he* gives into our hand the shield of faith, *he* sets upon our brow the helmet of salvation, *he* gives us the sword of the spirit in the right hand. It is the garment of Christ, the robe of his victory, that he puts upon his struggling community.

The Spirit teaches us that the time of temptations is not yet ended, but that the hardest temptation is still to come to his people. But he promises also: "Because thou didst keep the word of my patience, I also will keep thee from the hour of trial, that hour which is to come upon the whole world, to try them that dwell upon the earth. I come quickly" (Rev. 3:10ff.), and "The Lord knoweth how to deliver the godly out of temptation" (II Pet. 2:9).

So we pray, as Jesus Christ has taught us, to the Father in heaven: "Lead us not into temptation" and we know that our prayer is heard, for all temptation is conquered in Jesus Christ for all time, unto the end. So together with James we say: "Blessed is the man that endureth temptation, for when he hath been approved, he shall receive the crown of life, which the Lord promised to them that love him" (James 1:12). The promise of Jesus Christ proclaims: "Ye are they which have continued with me in my temptations, and I appoint unto you a kingdom" (Luke 22:28f.).

Protection and Help

...THE BIBLE teaches us in times of temptation in the flesh to *flee:* "Flee fornication" (I Cor. 6:18)—"from idolatry" (I Cor. 10:14)—"youthful lusts" (II Tim. 2:22)—"the lust of the world" (II Pet. 1:4). There is no resistance to Satan other than flight. Every struggle against lust in one's own strength is doomed to failure. Flee—that can indeed only mean, Flee to that place where you find protection and help, flee to the Crucified. His image and his presence alone can help. Here we see the crucified body and perceive in it the end of all desire; here we see right through Satan's deceit and here our spirit again becomes sober and aware of the enemy. Here I perceive the forsakenness and abandonment of my fleshly condition and the righteous judgement of God's wrath on all flesh. Here I know that in this lost condition I could never have helped myself against Satan, but that it is the victory of Jesus Christ which I now share. But here also I find ground for the attitude in which alone I can conquer all temptations—for patience (James 1:2ff.). I ought not to rebel against the temptations of the flesh in unlawful pride, as though I were too good for them. I ought to and I can humble myself under the hand of God and endure patiently the humiliation of such temptations. So I discern in the midst of Satan's deadly work the righteous and merciful punishment of God. In the death of Jesus I find refuge from Satan and the communion of death in the flesh under temptation and of life in the spirit through his victory.

Securitas

THE DEVIL tempts us in the sin of spiritual pride, in that he deceives us about the seriousness of God's law and of God's wrath. He takes the word of God's grace in his hand and whispers to us, God is a God of grace, he will not take our sins so seriously. So he awakens in us the longing to sin against God's grace and to assign forgiveness to ourselves even before our sin. He makes us secure in grace. We are God's children, we have Christ and his cross, we are the true church, no evil can now befall us. God will no longer hold us responsible for our sin. What spells ruin for others has no longer any danger for us. Through grace we have a privileged position before God. Here wanton sin threatens grace (Jude 4). Here it says: "Where is the God of judgement?" (Mal. 2:17), and "we call the proud happy; yea, they that work wickedness are built up; yea, they tempt God, and are delivered" (Mal. 3:15). From such talk follows all indolence of the spirit in prayer and in obedience, indifference to the Word of God, the deadening of conscience, the contempt of the good conscience, "shipwreck concerning the faith" (I Tim. 1:19). (Man persists in unforgiven sin and daily piles up guilt upon guilt.) Lastly there follows the complete hardening and obduracy of the heart in sin, in fearlessness and security before God, hypocritical piety (Acts 5:3 and 9). There is no longer any room for repentance, man can no longer obey. This way ends in idolatry. The God of grace has now become an idol which I serve. This is clearly the tempting of God which provokes the wrath of God.

Spiritual pride arises from disregard of the law and of

the wrath of God; whether I say that I am able to stand in my own goodness according to the law of God (justification by works); or whether I, through grace, bestow upon myself a privilege to sin (Nomism and Antinomianism). God is tempted in both, because I put to the test the seriousness of his wrath and demand a sign beyond his Word.

Tempted by Suffering

IF THE CHRISTIAN should fall into serious sickness, bitter poverty or other severe suffering, he should know that the devil has his hand in the game. Stoical resignation, which accepts everything as inevitable, is a self-defence of the man who will not acknowledge the devil and God. It has nothing to do with faith in God. The Christian knows that suffering in this world is linked with the fall of man, and that God does not will sickness, suffering and death. The Christian perceives in suffering a temptation of Satan to separate him from God. It is here that murmuring against God has its origin. While God disappears from man's sight in the fire of lust, the heat of affliction easily leads him into conflict with God. The Christian threatens to doubt the love of God. Why does God allow this suffering? God's justice is incomprehensible to him. Why must it happen to me? What have I done to deserve it? By suffering God should become our joy. Job is the Biblical prototype of this temptation. Everything is taken from Job by Satan, in order that in the end he may curse God. Violent pain, hunger and thirst can rob man of all his strength and lead him to the edge of apostasy.

How does the Christian conquer the temptation of

suffering? Here the end of the Book of Job is a great help to us. In the face of suffering Job has protested his innocence to the last, and has brushed aside the counsels to repentance from his friends who try to trace his misfortune back to a particular, perhaps hidden sin of Job. In addition, Job has spoken high-sounding words about his own righteousness. After the appearance of God Job declares: "Therefore have I uttered that which I understood not. . . . wherefore I abhor myself, and repent in dust and ashes" (Job, 42:3, 6). But the wrath of God is not now turned against Job, but against his friends: "for ye have not spoken of me the thing that is right, as my servant Job hath" (Job 42:7). Job gets justice before God and yet confesses his guilt before God. That is the solution of the problem. Job's suffering has its foundation not in his guilt but in his righteousness. Job is tempted because of his piety. So Job is right to protest against suffering coming upon him as if he were guilty. Yet this right comes to an end for Job when he no longer faces man but faces God. Face to face with God, even the good, innocent Job knows himself to be guilty.

This means for the Christian, tempted by suffering, that he must and should protest against suffering in so far as, in doing so, he protests against the devil and asserts his own innocence. The devil has broken into God's order and is the cause of suffering (Luther on Lenchen's death!). But in the presence of God the Christian also sees his sufferings as judgement on the sin of all flesh, which also dwells in his own flesh. He recognizes his sin and confesses himself to be guilty. "Thine own wickedness shall correct thee, and thy backslidings shall reprove thee. Know therefore and see that it is an evil thing and a bitter, that thou hast forsaken the Lord thy God, and that my fear is not in thee, saith the Lord, the Lord of hosts" (Jer. 2:19; 4:18). Suffering, therefore, leads to the knowledge of sin, and thereby, to the return to God. We see our suffering as the judgement of God on our flesh, and because of that we can be grateful for it. For judgement on the flesh, the death of the old man is only the side turned towards the world of the life of the new man. Thus it is said: "He that hath suffered in the flesh hath ceased from sin" (I Pet. 4:1). All suffering must lead the Christian to the strengthening of his faith and not to defection. While the flesh shuns suffering and rejects it, the Christian sees his suffering as the suffering of Christ in him. For he has borne our griefs and carried our sorrows. He bore God's wrath on sin. He died in the flesh, and so we also die in the flesh, because he lives in us.

Now the Christian understands his suffering, also, as the temptation of Christ in him. That leads him into patience, into the silent, waiting endurance of temptation, and fills him with gratitude; for the more the old man dies, the more certainly lives the new man; the deeper man is driven into suffering, the nearer he comes to Christ. Just because Satan took everything from Job, he cast him on God alone. So for the Christian suffering becomes a protest against the devil, a recognition of his own sin, the righteous judgement of God, the death of his old man, and communion with Jesus Christ.

Sorrow and Joy

SORROW and joy,
striking suddenly on our startled senses,
seem, at the first approach, all but impossible
of just distinction one from the other,
even as frost and heat at the first keen contact
burn us alike.

Joy and sorrow,
hurled from the height of heaven in meteor fashion,
flash in an arc of shining menace o'er us.
Those they touch are left
stricken amid the fragments
of their colourless, usual lives.

Imperturbable, mighty,
ruinous and compelling,
sorrow and joy
—summoned or all unsought for—
processionally enter.
Those they encounter
they transfigure, investing them
with strange gravity
and a spirit of worship.

Joy is rich in fears;
sorrow has its sweetness.
Indistinguishable from each other
they approach us from eternity,
equally potent in their power and terror.

From every quarter
mortals come hurrying,
part envious, part awe-struck,
swarming, and peering
into the portent,
where the mystery sent from above us
is transmuting into the inevitable
order of earthly human drama.

What, then, is joy? What, then, is sorrow?
Time alone can decide between them,
when the immediate poignant happening
lengthens out to continuous wearisome suffering,
when the laboured creeping moments of daylight
slowly uncover the fullness of our disaster,
sorrow's unmistakable features.

Then do most of our kind,
sated, if only by the monotony
of unrelieved unhappiness,
turn away from the drama, disillusioned,
uncompassionate.

O you mothers and loved ones—then, ah, then
comes your hour, the hour for true devotion.
Then your hour comes, you friends and brothers!
Loyal hearts can change the face of sorrow,
softly encircle it with love's most gentle
unearthly radiance.

Physical Suffering

I BELIEVE. . . that physical sufferings, actual pain and so on, are certainly to be classed as 'suffering'. We so like to stress spiritual suffering; and yet that is just what Christ is supposed to have taken from us, and I can find nothing about it in the New Testament, or in the acts of the early martyrs. After all, whether 'the church suffers' is not at all the same as whether one of its servants has to put up with this or that. I think we need a good deal of correction on this point; indeed, I must admit candidly that I sometimes feel almost ashamed of how often we've talked about our own sufferings. No, suffering must be something quite different, and have a quite different dimension, from what I've so far experienced.

Pain

STIFTER once said 'pain is a holy angel, who shows treasures to men which otherwise remain forever hidden; through him men have become greater than through all joys of the world.' It must be so and I tell this to myself in my present position over and over again—the pain of longing which often can be felt even physically, must be there, and we shall not and need not talk it away. But it needs to be overcome every time, and thus there is an even holier angel than the one of pain, that is the one of joy in God.

Prayers in Time of Distress

O LORD God,
great distress has come upon me;
my cares threaten to crush me,
and I do not know what to do.
O God, be gracious to me and help me.
Give me strength to bear what you send,
and do not let fear rule over me;
Take a father's care of my wife and children.

O merciful God,
forgive me all the sins that I have committed
against you and against my fellow men.
I trust in your grace
and commit my life wholly into your hands.
Do with me according to your will
and as is best for me.
Whether I live or die, I am with you,
and you, my God, are with me.
Lord, I wait for your salvation
and for your kingdom.
Amen.

Editor's note: Written for fellow prisoners Christmas 1943.

The Suffering Servant

WE KNOW full well that the marks of the passion, the wounds of the cross, are now become the marks of grace in the Body of the risen and glorified Christ. We know that the image of the Crucified lives henceforth in the glory of the eternal High Priest, who ever maketh intercession for us in Heaven. That Body, in which Christ had lived in the form of a servant, rose on Easter Day as a new Body, with heavenly form and radiance. But if we would have a share in that glory and radiance, we must first be conformed to the image of the Suffering Servant who was obedient to the death of the cross. If we would bear the image of his glory, we must first bear the image of his shame. There is no other way to recover the image we lost through the Fall.

The Suffering of the Messengers

NEITHER FAILURE NOR HOSTILITY can weaken the messenger's conviction that he has been sent by Jesus. That his word may be their strength, their stay and their comfort, Jesus repeats it. "Behold, I send you." For this is no way they have chosen themselves, no undertaking of their own. It is, in the strict sense of the word, a *mission*. With this the Lord promises them his abiding presence, even when they find themselves as sheep among wolves, defenceless, powerless, sore pressed and beset with great danger. Nothing can happen to them without Jesus knowing of it. "Be ye therefore wise as serpents, and harmless as doves." How often have the ministers of Jesus made wrong use of this saying! However willing they may be, it is indeed difficult for them to preserve a true understanding of this word, and to adhere to the path of obedience. How difficult it is to draw the line with certainty between spiritual wisdom and worldly astuteness! Are we not all prepared at heart to do without "worldly wisdom" and much prefer the harmlessness of the doves and thus again fall into disobedience? Who is there to let us know when we are running away from suffering through cowardice, or running after it through temerity? Who shows us the hidden frontier? It is just as bad to appeal to the commandment of simplicity against that of wisdom, as to appeal to the commandment of wisdom against that of simplicity. There is one in the world who has a perfect knowledge of his own heart. But Jesus never called his disciples into a state of uncertainty, but to one of supreme certainty. That is why his warning can only summon them to abide by the Word. Where the Word is, there shall the disciple be. Therein lies his true wisdom and his true simplicity. If it is obvious that the Word is being rejected, if it is forced to yield its ground, the disciple must yield with it. But if the Word carries on the battle, the disciple must also stand his ground.

Sharing in God's Sufferings

...THE CHRISTIAN is not a *homo religiosus*, but simply a man, as Jesus was a man—in contrast, shall we say, to John the Baptist. I don't mean the shallow and banal this-worldliness of the enlightened, the busy, the comfortable, or the lascivious, but the profound this-worldliness, characterized by discipline and the constant knowledge of death and resurrection. I think Luther lived a this-worldly life in this sense.

I remember a conversation that I had in America thirteen years ago with a young French pastor.[1] We were asking ourselves quite simply what we wanted to do with our lives. He said he would like to become a saint (and I think it's quite likely that he did become one). At the time I was very impressed, but I disagreed with him, and said, in effect, that I should like to learn to have faith. For a long time I didn't realize the depth of the contrast. I thought I could acquire faith by trying to live a holy life, or something like it. I suppose I wrote *The Cost of Discipleship* as the end of that path. Today I can see the dangers of that book, though I still stand by what I wrote.

I discovered later, and I'm still discovering right up to this moment, that it is only by living completely in this world that one learns to have faith. One must completely abandon any attempt to make something of oneself, whether it be a saint, or a converted sinner, or a churchman (a so-called priestly type!), a righteous man or an unrighteous one, a sick man or a healthy one. By this-

---

[1]Jean Lasserre.

worldliness I mean living unreservedly in life's duties, problems, successes and failures, experiences and perplexities. In so doing we throw ourselves completely into the arms of God, taking seriously, not our own sufferings, but those of God in the world—watching with Christ in Gethsemane. That, I think, is faith; that is *metanoia*; and that is how one becomes a man and a Christian (cf. Jer. 45!). How can success make us arrogant, or failure lead us astray, when we share in God's sufferings through a life of this kind?

Night Voices in Tegel

STRETCHED OUT on my cot
I stare at the grey wall.
Outside, a summer evening
That does not know me
Goes singing into the countryside.
Slowly and softly
The tides of the day ebb
On the eternal shore.
Sleep a little,
Strengthen body and soul, head and hand,
For peoples, houses, spirits and hearts
Are aflame.
Till your day breaks
After blood-red night—
Stand fast!

Night and silence.
I listen.
Only the steps and cries of the guards,
The distant, hidden laughter of two lovers.
Do you hear nothing else, lazy sleeper?

I hear my own soul tremble and heave.
Nothing else?
I hear, I hear
The silent night thoughts
Of my fellow sufferers asleep or awake,
As if voices, cries,

As if shouts for planks to save them.
I hear the uneasy creak of the beds,
I hear chains.

I hear how sleepless men toss and turn,
Who long for freedom and deeds of wrath.
When at grey dawn sleep finds them
They murmur in dreams of their wives and children.

I hear the happy lisp of half-grown boys,
Delighting in childhood dreams;
I hear them tug at their blankets
And hide from hideous nightmares.

I hear the sighs and weak breath of the old,
Who in silence prepare for the last journey.
They have seen justice and injustice come and go;
Now they wish to see the imperishable, the eternal.

Night and silence.
Only the steps and cries of the guards.
Do you hear how in the silent house
It quakes, cracks, roars
When hundreds kindle the stirred-up flame of their
    hearts?

Their choir is silent,
But my ear is open wide:
'We the old, the young,
The sons of all tongues,
We the strong, the weak,
The sleepers, the wakeful,
We the poor, the rich,
Alike in misfortune,

The good, the bad,
Whatever we have been,
We men of many scars,
We the witnesses of those who died,
We the defiant, we the despondent,
The innocent, and the much accused,
Deeply tormented by long isolation,
Brother, we are searching, we are calling you!
Brother, do you hear me?'

Twelve cold, thin strokes of the tower clock
Awaken me.
No sound, no warmth in them
To hide and cover me.
Howling, evil dogs at midnight
Frighten me.
The wretched noise
Divides a poor yesterday
From a poor today.
What can it matter to me
Whether one day turns into another,
One that could have nothing new, nothing better
Than to end quickly like this one?
I want to see the turning of the times,
When luminous signs stand in the night sky,
And over the peoples new bells
Ring and ring.
I am waiting for that midnight
In whose fearfully streaming brilliance
The evil perish for anguish
And the good overcome with joy.

The villain
Comes to light
In the judgement.

Deceit and betrayal,
Malicious deeds—
Atonement is near.

See, O man,
Holy strength
Is at work, setting right.

Rejoice and proclaim
Faithfulness and right
For a new race!

Heaven, reconcile
The sons of earth
To peace and beauty.

Earth, flourish;
Man, become free,
Be free!

Suddenly I sat up,
As if, from a sinking ship, I had sighted land,
As if there were something to grasp, to seize,
As if I saw golden fruit ripen.
But wherever I look, grasp, or seize,
There is only the impenetrable mass of darkness.

I sink into brooding;
I sink myself into the depths of the dark.
You night, full of outrage and evil,
Make yourself known to me!
Why and for how long will you try our patience?
A deep and long silence;
Then I hear the night bend down to me:
'I am not dark; only guilt is dark!'

Guilt! I hear a trembling and quaking,
A murmur, a lament that arises;
I hear men grow angry in spirit.
In the wild uproar of innumerable voices
A silent chorus
Assails God's ear:

'Pursued and hunted by men,
Made defenceless and accused,
Bearers of unbearable burdens,
We are yet the accusers.

'We accuse those who plunged us into sin,
Who made us share the guilt,
Who made us the witnesses of injustice,
In order to despise their accomplices.

'Our eyes had to see folly,
In order to bind us in deep guilt;
Then they stopped our mouths,
And we were as dumb dogs.

'We learned to lie easily,
To be at the disposal of open injustice;
If the defenceless was abused,
Then our eyes remained cold.

'And that which burned in our hearts,
Remained silent and unnamed;
We quenched our fiery blood
And stamped out the inner flame.

'The once holy bonds uniting men
Were mangled and flayed,

Friendship and faithfulness betrayed;
Tears and rue were reviled.

'We sons of pious races,
One-time defenders of right and truth,
Became despisers of God and man,
Amid hellish laughter.

'Yet though now robbed of freedom and honour,
We raise our heads proudly before men.
And if we are brought into disrepute,
Before men we declare our innocence.

'Steady and firm we stand man against man;
As the accused we accuse!

'Only before thee, source of all being,
Before thee are we sinners.

'Afraid of suffering and poor in deeds,
We have betrayed thee before men.

'We saw the lie raise its head,
And we did not honour the truth.

'We saw brethren in direst need,
And feared only our own death.

'We come before thee as men,
As confessors of our sins.

'Lord, after the ferment of these times,
Send us times of assurance.

'After so much going astray,
Let us see the day break.

'Let there be ways built for us by thy word
As far as eye can see.

'Until thou wipe out our guilt,
Keep us in quiet patience.

'We will silently prepare ourselves,
Till thou dost call to new times.

'Until thou stillest storm and flood,
And thy will does wonders.

'Brother, till the night be past,
Pray for me!'

The first light of morning creeps through my window
    pale and grey,
A light, warm summer wind blows over my brow.
'Summer day,' I will only say, 'beautiful summer
    day!'
What may it bring to me?
Then I hear outside hasty, muffled steps;
Near me they stop suddenly.
I turn cold and hot,
For I know, oh, I know!
A soft voice reads something cuttingly and cold.
Control yourself, brother; soon you will have finished it,
soon, soon.
I hear you stride bravely and with proud step.
You no longer see the present, you see the future.
I go with you, brother, to that place,
And I hear your last word:
'Brother, when the sun turns pale for me,
Then live for me.'

Stretched out on my cot
I stare at the grey wall.
Outside a summer morning
Which is not yet mine
Goes brightly into the countryside.

Brother, till after the long night
Our day breaks
We stand fast!

Separation from Those We Love

FIRST: nothing can make up for the absence of someone whom we love, and it would be wrong to try to find a substitute; we must simply hold out and see it through. That sounds very hard at first, but at the same time it is a great consolation, for the gap, as long as it remains unfilled, preserves the bonds between us. It is nonsense to say that God fills the gap; he doesn't fill it, but on the contrary, he keeps it empty and so helps us to keep alive our former communion with each other, even at the cost of pain.

Secondly: the dearer and richer our memories, the more difficult the separation. But gratitude changes the pangs of memory into a tranquil joy. The beauties of the past are borne, not as a thorn in the flesh, but as a precious gift in themselves. We must take care not to wallow in our memories or hand ourselves over to them, just as we do not gaze all the time at a valuable present, but only at special times, and apart from these keep it simply as a hidden treasure that is ours for certain. In this way the past gives us lasting joy and strength.

Thirdly: times of separation are not a total loss or unprofitable for our companionship, or at any rate they need not be so. In spite of all the difficulties that they bring, they can be the means of strengthening fellowship quite remarkably.

Fourthly: I've learnt here especially that the *facts* can always be mastered, and that difficulties are magnified out of all proportion simply by fear and anxiety. From the moment we wake until we fall asleep we must commend other people wholly and unreservedly to God and leave them in his hands, and transform our anxiety for them into prayers on their behalf:

> With sorrow and with grief...
> God *will not* be distracted.

Christ's Restoration

> Let pass, dear brothers, every pain;
> What you have missed I'll bring again.

WHAT DOES THIS 'I'll bring again' mean? It means that nothing is lost, that everything is taken up in Christ, although it is transformed, made transparent, clear, and free from all selfish desire. Christ restores all this as God originally intended it to be, without the distortion resulting from our sins. The doctrine derived from Eph. 1:10— that of the restoration of all things, ἀνακεφαλαίωσις, *recapitulatio* (Irenaeus)—is a magnificent conception, full of comfort. This is how the promise 'God seeks what has been driven away' is fulfilled. And no one has expressed this so simply and artlessly as Paul Gerhardt in these

words that he puts into the mouth of the Christ-child: 'I'll
bring again'. Perhaps this line will help you a little in the
coming weeks. Besides that, I've lately learnt for the first
time to appreciate the hymn 'Beside thy cradle here I
stand'. Up to now I hadn't made much of it; I suppose one
has to be alone for a long time, and meditate on it, to be
able to take it in properly. Every word is remarkably full of
meaning and beauty. There's just a slight flavour of the
monastery and mysticism, but no more than is justified.
After all, it's right to speak of 'I' and 'Christ' as well as of
'we', and what that means can hardly be expressed better
than it is in this hymn. There are also a few passages in a
similar vein in the *Imitation of Christ*, which I'm reading
now and then in the Latin (it reads much better in Latin
than in German); and I sometimes think of

from the Augustinian *O bone Jesu* by Schütz. Doesn't this
passage, in its ecstatic longing combined with pure
devotion, suggest the 'bringing again' of all earthly desire?
'Bringing again' mustn't, of course, be confused with
'sublimation'; 'sublimation' is σάρξ 'flesh' (and pietistic?),
and 'restoration' is spirit, not in the sense of 'spiritualiza-
tion' (which is also σάρξ), but of καινὴ κτίσις through the
πνεῦμα ἅγιον, a new creation through the Holy Spirit. I
think this point is also very important when we have to
talk to people who ask us about their relation to their
dead. '*I* will bring again'—that is, we cannot and should
not take it back ourselves, but allow Christ to give it back
to us.

New Year 1945

WITH EVERY POWER for good to stay and guide me,
comforted and inspired beyond all fear,
I'll live these days with you in thought beside me,
and pass, with you, into the coming year.

The old year still torments our hearts, unhastening:
the long days of our sorrow still endure.
Father, grant to the soul thou hast been chastening
that thou hast promised—the healing and the cure.

Should it be ours to drain the cup of grieving
even to the dregs of pain, at thy command,
we will not falter, thankfully receiving
all that is given by thy loving hand.

But, should it be thy will once more to release us
to life's enjoyment and its good sunshine,
that we've learned from sorrow shall increase us
and all our life be dedicate as thine.

To-day, let candles shed their radiant greeting:
lo, on our darkness are they not thy light,
leading us haply to our longed-for meeting?
Thou canst illumine e'en our darkest night.

Editor's note: Composed during heavy air raids at the Gestapo prison in Berlin. Translated by Geoffrey Winthrop Young.

When now the silence deepens for our harkening,
grant we may hear thy children's voices raise
from all the unseen world around us darkening
their universal paean, in thy praise.

While all the powers of Good aid and attend us,
boldly we'll face the future, be it what may.
At even, and at morn, God will befriend us,
And oh, most surely on each new year's day!

Glorifying God

...PSALM 50 says quite clearly, 'Call upon me in the day of trouble; I will deliver you, and you shall glorify me.' The whole history of the children of Israel consists of such cries for help. And I must say that the last two nights have made me face this problem again in a quite elementary way. While the bombs are falling like that all round the building, I cannot help thinking of God, his judgement, his hand stretched out and his anger not turned away (Isa. 5:25 and 9:11–10:4), and of my own unpreparedness. I feel how men can make vows, and then I think of you all and say, 'better me than one of them'—and that makes me realize how attached I am to you all. I won't say anything more about it—it will have to be by word of mouth; but when all is said and done, it's true that it needs trouble to shake us up and drive us to prayer, though I feel every time that it is something to be ashamed of, as indeed it is. That may be because I haven't so far felt able to say a Christian word to the others at such a moment. As we were again lying on the floor last night, and someone exclaimed 'O God, O God' (he is normally a very flippant type), I couldn't bring myself to offer him any Christian encouragement or comfort; all I did was to look at my watch and say, 'It won't last more than ten minutes now.' There was nothing premeditated about it; it came quite automatically, and perhaps I felt that it was wrong to force religion down his throat just then. (Incidentally, Jesus didn't try to convert the two thieves on the cross; one of them turned to him!)

Call of Liberation

...MAN CANNOT LIVE simultaneously in reconciliation and in disunion, in freedom and under the law, in simplicity and in discordancy. There are no transitions or intermediate stages here; it is one thing or the other. But it is impossible for a man by his own power to void and to overcome his knowledge of his own goodness, though he may deceive himself and mistake the methodical repression of this knowledge for the actual overcoming of it. That is why when Jesus speaks of the right hand which must not know what the left hand is doing, in other words of the concealment of a man's own goodness, it is once again the summons to forsake disunion, apostasy and the knowledge of good and evil, and to return to unity and to the origin, to the new life which is in Jesus alone. It is the call of liberation, the call to simplicity and to conversion; it is the call which nullifies the old knowledge of the apostasy and which imparts the new knowledge of Jesus, that knowledge which is entirely contained in the doing of the will of God. . . .

Freedom

RESPONSIBILITY AND FREEDOM are corresponding concepts. Factually, though not chronologically, responsibility presupposes freedom and freedom can consist only in responsibility. Responsibility is the freedom of men which is given only in the obligation to God and to our neighbour.

The responsible man acts in the freedom of his own self, without the support of men, circumstances or principles, but with a due consideration for the given human and general conditions and for the relevant questions of principle. The proof of his freedom is the fact that nothing can answer for him, nothing can exonerate him, except his own deed and his own self. It is he himself who must observe, judge, weigh up, decide and act. It is man himself who must examine the motives, the prospects, the value and the purpose of his action. But neither the purity of the motivation, nor the opportune circumstances, nor the value, nor the significant purpose of an intended undertaking can become the governing law of his action, a law to which he can withdraw, to which he can appeal as an authority, and by which he can be exculpated and acquitted.[1] For in that case he would indeed no longer be truly free. The action of the responsible man is performed in the obligation which alone gives freedom and which gives entire freedom, the obligation to God and to our neighbour as they confront us in Jesus Christ. At the same time it is performed wholly within the domain of relativ-

---

[1]This makes it unnecessary to raise the fallacious question of determinism and indeterminism, in which the essence of mental decision is incorrectly substituted for the law of causality.

ity, wholly in the twilight which the historical situation spreads over good and evil; it is performed in the midst of the innumerable perspectives in which every given phenomenon appears. It has not to decide simply between right and wrong and between good and evil, but between right and right and between wrong and wrong. As Aeschylus said, 'right strives with right'. Precisely in this respect responsible action is a free venture; it is not justified by any law; it is performed without any claim to a valid self-justification, and therefore also without any claim to an ultimate valid knowledge of good and evil. Good, as what is responsible, is performed in ignorance of good and in the surrender to God of the deed which has become necessary and which is nevertheless, or for that very reason, free; for it is God who sees the heart, who weighs up the deed, and who directs the course of history.

Stations on the Road to Freedom

Discipline

If you set out to seek freedom, then learn above all
　things
to govern your soul and your senses, for fear that
　your passions
and longing may lead you away from the path you
　should follow.
Chaste be your mind and your body, and both in
　subjection,
obediently, steadfastly seeking the aim set before
　them;
only through discipline may a man learn to be free.

Action

Daring to do what is right, not what fancy may tell
　you,
valiantly grasping occasions, not cravenly doubting—
freedom comes only through deeds, not through
　thoughts taking wing.
Faint not nor fear, but go out to the storm and the
　action,
trusting in God whose commandment you faithfully
　follow;
freedom, exultant, will welcome your joy.

Suffering

A change has come indeed. Your hands, so strong
    and active,
are bound; in helplessness now you see your action
is ended; you sigh in relief, your cause committing
to stronger hands; so now you may rest contented.
Only for one blissful moment could you draw near to
    touch freedom;
then, that it might be perfected in glory, you gave it to
    God.

Death

Come now, thou greatest of feasts on the journey to
    freedom eternal;
death, cast aside all the burdensome chains, and
    demolish
the walls of our temporal body, the walls of our souls
    that are blinded,
so that at last we may see that which here remains
    hidden.
Freedom, how long we have sought thee in disci-
    pline, action, and suffering;
dying, we now may behold thee revealed in the Lord.

Obedience and Freedom

...JESUS STANDS BEFORE GOD as the one who is both obedient and free. As the obedient one He does His Father's will in blind compliance with the law which is commanded Him, and as the free one He acquiesces in God's will out of His own most personal knowledge, with open eyes and a joyous heart; He re-creates this will, as it were, out of Himself. Obedience without freedom is slavery; freedom without obedience is arbitrary self-will. Obedience restrains freedom; and freedom ennobles obedience. Obedience binds the creature to the Creator and freedom enables the creature to stand before the Creator as one who is made in His image. Obedience shows man that he must allow himself to be told what is good and what God requires of him (Micah 6:8); and liberty enables him to do good himself. Obedience knows what is good and does it, and freedom dares to act, and abandons to God the judgement of good and evil. Obedience follows blindly and freedom has open eyes. Obedience acts without questioning and freedom asks what is the purpose. Obedience has its hands tied and freedom is creative. In obedience man adheres to the decalogue and in freedom man creates new decalogues (Luther).

In responsibility both obedience and freedom are realized. Responsibility implies tension between obedience and freedom. There would be no more responsibility if either were made independent of the other. Responsible action is subject to obligation, and yet it is creative. To make obedience independent of freedom leads only to the Kantian ethic of duty, and to make freedom independent

194 · THE MARTYRED CHRISTIAN

of obedience leads only to the ethic of irresponsible genius. Both the man of duty and the genius carry their justification within themselves. The man of responsibility stands between obligation and freedom; he must dare to act under obligation and in freedom; yet he finds his justification neither in his obligation nor in his freedom but solely in Him who has put him in this (humanly impossible) situation and who requires this deed of him. The responsible man delivers up himself and his deed to God.

The World of Conflicts

THE KNOWLEDGE of good and evil seems to be the aim of all ethical reflection.[1] The first task of Christian ethics is to invalidate this knowledge. In launching this attack on the underlying assumptions of all other ethics, Christian ethics stands so completely alone that it becomes questionable whether there is any purpose in speaking of Christian ethics at all. But if one does so notwithstanding, that can only mean that Christian ethics claims to discuss the origin of the whole problem of ethics, and thus professes to be a critique of all ethics simply as ethics.

Already in the possibility of the knowledge of good and evil Christian ethics discerns a falling away from the origin. Man at his origin knows only one thing: God. It is only in the unity of his knowledge of God that he knows

---

[1]For the purposes of our present discussion it makes no difference if modern ethics replaces the concepts of good and evil by those of moral and immoral, valuable and valueless or (in the case of existential philosophy) of actual or proper being and not actual or proper being.

of other men, of things, and of himself. He knows all things only in God, and God in all things. The knowledge of good and evil shows that he is no longer at one with this origin.

In the knowledge of good and evil man does not understand himself in the reality of the destiny appointed in his origin, but rather in his own possibilities, his possibility of being good or evil. He knows himself now as something apart from God, outside God, and this means that he now knows only himself and no longer knows God at all; for he can know God only if he knows only God. The knowledge of good and evil is therefore separation from God. Only against God can man know good and evil.

Contempt for Humanity?

THERE IS A VERY REAL DANGER of our drifting into an attitude of contempt for humanity. We know quite well that we have no right to do so, and that it would lead us into the most sterile relation to our fellow-men. The following thoughts may keep us from such a temptation. It means that we at once fall into the worst blunders of our opponents. The man who despises another will never be able to make anything of him. Nothing that we despise in the other man is entirely absent from ourselves. We often expect from others more than we are willing to do ourselves. Why have we hitherto thought so intemperately about man and his frailty and temptability? We must learn to regard people less in the light of what they do or omit to do, and more in the light of what they suffer. The only profitable relationship to others—and especially to our weaker brethren—is one of love, and that means the will to hold fellowship with them. God himself did not despise humanity, but became man for men's sake.

Immanent Righteousness

IT IS ONE OF THE MOST SURPRISING experiences, but at the same time one of the most incontrovertible, that evil—often in a surprisingly short time—proves its own folly and defeats its own object. That does not mean that punishment follows hard on the heels of every evil action; but it does mean that deliberate transgression of the divine law in the supposed interests of worldly self-preservation has exactly the opposite effect. We learn this from our own experience, and we can interpret it in various ways. At least it seems possible to infer with certainty that in social life there are laws more powerful than anything that may claim to dominate them, and that it is therefore not only wrong but unwise to disregard them. We can understand from this why Aristotelian–Thomist ethics made wisdom one of the cardinal virtues. Wisdom and folly are not ethically indifferent, as Neo-protestant motive-ethics would have it. In the fullness of the concrete situation and the possibilities which it offers, the wise man at the same time recognizes the impassable limits that are set to all action by the permanent laws of human social life; and in this knowledge the wise man acts well and the good man wisely.

It is true that all historically important action is constantly overstepping the limits set by these laws. But it makes all the difference whether such overstepping of the appointed limits is regarded in principle as the superseding of them, and is therefore given out to be a law of a special kind, or whether the overstepping is deliberately regarded as a fault which is perhaps unavoidable, justified only if the law and the limit are re-established and respected as soon as possible. It is not necessarily hypocrisy if the declared aim of political action is the restoration of the law, and not mere self-preservation. The world *is*, in fact, so ordered that a basic respect for ultimate laws and human life is also the best means of self-preservation, and that these laws may be broken only on the odd occasion in case of brief necessity, whereas anyone who turns necessity into a principle, and in so doing establishes a law of his own alongside them, is inevitably bound, sooner or later, to suffer retribution. The immanent righteousness of history rewards and punishes only men's deeds, but the eternal righteousness of God tries and judges their hearts.

The Sense of Quality

UNLESS WE HAVE THE COURAGE to fight for a revival of wholesome reserve between man and man, we shall perish in an anarchy of human values. The impudent contempt for such reserve is the mark of the rabble, just as inward uncertainty, haggling and cringing for the favour of insolent people, and lowering oneself to the level of the rabble are the way of becoming no better than the rabble oneself. When we forget what is due to ourselves and to others, when the feeling for human quality and the power to exercise reserve cease to exist, chaos is at the door. When we tolerate impudence for the sake of material comforts, then we abandon our self-respect, the floodgates are opened, chaos bursts the dam that we were to defend; and we are responsible for it all. In other times it may have been the business of Christianity to champion the equality of all men; its business today will be to defend passionately human dignity and reserve. The misinterpretation that we are acting for our own interests, and the cheap insinuation that our attitude is anti-social, we shall simply have to put up with; they are the invariable protests of the rabble against decency and order. Anyone who is pliant and uncertain in this matter does not realize what is at stake, and indeed in his case the reproaches may well be justified. We are witnessing the levelling down of all ranks of society, and at the same time the birth of a new sense of nobility, which is binding together a circle of men from all former social classes. Nobility arises from and exists by sacrifice, courage, and a clear sense of duty to oneself and society, by expecting due regard for itself as a matter of course; and it shows an equally natural regard for others, whether they are of higher or of lower degree. We need all along the line to recover the lost sense of quality and social order based on quality. Quality is the greatest enemy of any kind of mass-levelling. Socially it means the renunciation of all place-hunting, a break with the cult of the 'star', an open eye both upwards and downwards, especially in the choice of one's more intimate friends, and pleasure in private life as well as courage to enter public life. Culturally it means a return from the newspaper and the radio to the book, from feverish activity to unhurried leisure, from dispersion to concentration, from sensationalism to reflection, from virtuosity to art, from snobbery to modesty, from extravagance to moderation. Quantities are competitive, qualities are complementary.

The Penultimate

IN JESUS CHRIST we have faith in the incarnate, crucified and risen God. In the incarnation we learn of the love of God for His creation; in the crucifixion we learn of the judgement of God upon all flesh; and in the resurrection we learn of God's will for a new world. There could be no greater error than to tear these three elements apart; for each of them comprises the whole. It is quite wrong to establish a separate theology of the incarnation, a theology of the cross, or a theology of the resurrection, each in opposition to the others, by a misconceived absolutization of one of these parts; it is equally wrong to apply the same procedure to a consideration of the Christian life. A Christian ethic constructed solely on the basis of the incarnation would lead directly to the compromise solution. An ethic which was based solely on the cross or the resurrection of Jesus would fall victim to radicalism and enthusiasm. Only in the unity is the conflict resolved.

Jesus Christ the man—this means that God enters into created reality. It means that we have the right and the obligation to be men before God. The destruction of manhood, of man's quality as man (*Menschsein*), is sin, and is therefore a hindrance to God's redemption of man. Yet the manhood (*Menschsein*) of Jesus Christ does not mean simply the corroboration of the established world and of the human character as it is. Jesus was man 'without sin' (Heb. 4:15); that is what is decisive. Yet among men Jesus lived in the most utter poverty, unmarried, and He died as a criminal. Thus the manhood of Jesus implies already a twofold condemnation of man, the absolute condemnation of sin and the relative condemnation of the established human orders. But even under this condemnation Jesus is really man, and it is His will that we shall be men. He neither renders the human reality independent nor destroys it, but He allows it to remain as that which is before the last, as a penultimate which requires to be taken seriously in its own way, and yet not to be taken seriously, a penultimate which has become the outer covering of the ultimate.

The Sovereignty of God in History

I BELIEVE that God can and will bring good out of evil, even out of the greatest evil. For that purpose he needs men who make the best use of everything. I believe that God will give us all the strength we need to help us to resist in all time of distress. But he never gives it in advance, lest we should rely on ourselves and not on him alone. A faith such as this should allay all our fears for the future. I believe that even our mistakes and shortcomings are turned to good account, and that it is no harder for God to deal with them than with our supposedly good deeds. I believe that God is no timeless fate, but that he waits for and answers sincere prayers and responsible actions.

Present and Future

WE USED TO THINK that one of the inalienable rights of man was that he should be able to plan both his professional and his private life. That is a thing of the past. The force of circumstances has brought us into a situation where we have to give up being 'anxious about tomorrow' (Matt. 6:34). But it makes all the difference whether we accept this willingly and in faith (as the Sermon on the Mount intends), or under continual constraint. For most people, the compulsory abandonment of planning for the future means that they are forced back into living just for the moment, irresponsibly, frivolously, or resignedly; some few dream longingly of better times to come, and try to forget the present. We find both these courses equally impossible, and there remains for us only the very narrow way, often extremely difficult to find, of living every day as if it were our last, and yet living in faith and responsibility as though there were to be a great future: 'Houses and fields and vineyards shall again be bought in this land' proclaims Jeremiah (32:15), in paradoxical contrast to his prophecies of woe, just before the destruction of the holy city. It is a sign from God and a pledge of a fresh start and a great future, just when all seems black. Thinking and acting for the sake of the coming generation, but being ready to go any day without fear or anxiety—that, in practice, is the spirit in which we are forced to live. It is not easy to be brave and keep that spirit alive, but it is imperative.

Editor's note: Written during resistance to Hitler.

Christ and Antichrist

THE OLDER THE WORLD GROWS, the more heated becomes the conflict between Christ and Antichrist, and the more thorough the efforts of the world to get rid of the Christians. Until now the world had always granted them a lodging-place by allowing them to work for their own food and clothing. . . . When the Christian community has been deprived of its last inch of space on the earth, the end will be near.

Thus while it is true that the Body of Christ makes a deep invasion into the sphere of secular life, yet at the same time the great gulf between the two is always clear at other points, and must become increasingly so. But whether in the world or out of it, the Christian's choice is determined by obedience to the same word: "Be not fashioned according to this world: but be ye transformed (μεταμορφοῦσθε) by the renewing of your mind, that ye may prove what is the good and acceptable and perfect will of God" (Rom. 12:2). There is a way of putting oneself on the same level as the world in the world as there is a way of creating one's own spiritual "world" in a monastery. There is a wrong way of staying in the world and a wrong way of fleeing from it. In both cases we are fashioning ourselves according to the world. But the Church of Christ has a different "form" from the world. Her task is increasingly to realize this form. It is the form of Christ himself, who came into the world and of his infinite mercy bore mankind and took it to himself, but who notwithstanding did not fashion himself in accordance with it but was rejected and cast out by it. He was not of this world. In the right confrontation with the world, the Church will become ever more like to the form of its suffering Lord.

Justification as the Last Word

THE ORIGIN and the essence of all Christian life are comprised in the one process or event which the Reformation called justification of the sinner by grace alone. The nature of the Christian life is disclosed not by what the man is in himself but by what he is in this event. The whole length and breadth of human life is here compressed into a single instant, a single point. The totality of life is encompassed in this event. What event is this? It is something final, something which cannot be grasped by the being or the action or the suffering of any man. The dark pit of human life, inwardly and outwardly barred, sinking ever more hopelessly and inescapably in the abyss, is torn open by main force, and the word of God breaks in. In the rescuing light man for the first time recognizes God and his neighbour. The labyrinth of the life he has so far led falls in ruin. Man is free for God and his brothers. He becomes aware that there is a God who loves him; that a brother is standing at his side, whom God loves as he loves him himself and that there is a future with the triune God, together with His Church. He believes. He loves. He hopes. The past and the future of his whole life are merged in one in the presence of God. The whole of the past is comprised in the word forgiveness. The whole of the future is in safe keeping in the faithfulness of God. Past sin is swallowed up in the abyss of the love of God in Jesus Christ. The future will be without sin, a life which proceeds from God (I John 3:9). Life knows now that it is held in tension between the two poles of eternity, that it extends from the choice made before the time of the world to the everlasting salvation. It knows itself to be a member of a Church and a creation which sings the praise of the triune God. All this takes place when Christ comes to men. In Christ all this is truth and reality, and just because it is not a dream, the life of the man who experiences the presence of Christ is henceforward no longer a lost life, but it has become a justified life, a life justified by grace alone.

Yet not only by grace alone, but also by faith alone. That is the teaching of the Bible and of the Reformation. A life is not justified by love or by hope, but only by faith. For indeed faith alone sets life upon a new foundation, and it is this new foundation alone that justifies my being able to live before God. This foundation is the life, the death and the resurrection of the Lord Jesus Christ. Without this foundation a life is unjustified before God. It is delivered up to death and damnation. To live by the life, the death and the resurrection of Jesus Christ is the justification of a life before God. And faith means the finding and holding fast of this foundation.

Blessing and Completion

IN THE BIBLE "rest" really means more than "having a rest." It means rest after the work is accomplished, it means completion, it means the perfection and peace of God in which the world rests, it means transfiguration, it means turning our eyes absolutely upon God's being God and towards worshipping him. It is never the rest of a lethargic God; it is the rest of the Creator. It is no relinquishing of the world, but the ultimate glorification of the world which is gazing upon the Creator. God must remain the Creator in his rest, too; "my Father worketh hitherto, and I work." God remains the Creator, but now as the one who has accomplished his work. We now understand God's rest to be at the same time the rest of his creation. His rest is our rest (as his freedom is our freedom, his goodness our goodness). Therefore God sanctifies the day of his rest for Adam and for us, whose heart is restless until it finds rest in God's rest. As far as we are concerned this rest is the promise which has been given to the people of God. It is unbelieving insolence either to want to snatch God's peace for ourselves prematurely in pious quietism or to reason impudently about the boredom of the peace of paradise, thereby combining and glorifying unrest and battle. This loud pleasure in one's own personal vitality might have to grow silent very quickly in the presence of the "living" God.

It is the day which in the New Testament is the day of the Lord's resurrection. It is the day of rest, the day of victory, of dominion, of perfection, of transfiguration; for us, the day of worship, the day of hope looking towards the day of final rest with God, the "rest of the people." All the days of the week have really only been created for its sake. Thou shalt keep holy the holiday and not sleep it away. For the sake of the final rest, for the sake of the resurrection of Jesus Christ, for the sake of the day of the final resurrection and the rest of the Creator with his creatures everything has been created, we have been created "that they may rest from their labours, for their works follow with them."

Jonah

'O GODS ETERNAL, excellent, provoked to anger,
help us, or give a sign, that we may know
who has offended you by secret sin,
by breach of oath, or heedless blasphemy, or murder,

who brings us to disaster by misdeed still hidden,
to make a paltry profit for his pride.'
Thus they besought. And Jonah said, 'Behold,
I sinned before the Lord of hosts. My life is forfeit.

Cast me away! My guilt must bear the wrath of God;
the righteous shall not perish with the sinner!'
They trembled. But with hands that knew no
     weakness
they cast the offender from their midst. The sea stood
     still.

In fear of death they cried aloud and, clinging fast
to wet ropes straining on the battered deck,
they gazed in stricken terror at the sea
that now, unchained in sudden fury, lashed the ship.

Editor's note: This poem was written after a plan to escape had been
abandoned.

The Last Temptation

...THE LAST ENEMY is death. Death is in Satan's hands. The sinner dies. Death is the last temptation. But even here where man loses everything, where hell reveals its terror, even here life has broken in upon the believer. Satan loses his last power and his last right over the believer. We ask once more: Why does God give Satan opportunity for temptation? First, in order finally to overcome Satan. Through getting his rights Satan is destroyed. As God punishes the godless man by allowing him to be godless, and allowing him his right and his freedom, and as the godless man perishes in this freedom of his (Rom. 1:19ff.), so God does not destroy Satan by an act of violence, but Satan must destroy himself. Second, God gives opportunity to Satan in order to bring believers to salvation. Only by knowledge of sin, by suffering and death, can the new man live. Third, the overcoming of Satan and the salvation of believers is true and real in Jesus Christ alone. Satan plagues Jesus with all sins, all suffering and the death of mankind. But with that his power is at an end. He had taken everything from Jesus Christ and thereby delivered him to God alone. Thus we are led to the knowledge from which we set out: Believers must learn to understand all their temptations as the temptation of Jesus Christ in them. In this way they will share in the victory.

The Last Judgement

...WHEN JESUS sits in judgement His own will not know that they have given Him food and drink and clothing and comfort. They will not know their own goodness; Jesus will disclose it to them. Then the time will have come for which there was no time here on earth, the time which will lay bare what is concealed so that it may then receive its public reward, the time of judgement. But even then all judging and all knowing will be on the part of God and of Jesus Christ, and we ourselves shall be filled with wonder at what we receive. The Pharisee, who thought that through impartial and earnest judgement of himself he could anticipate and prepare for the last judgement, cannot but regard as unintelligible and wrongful the message that he is to receive goodness solely from the knowledge, from the judgement and from the hand of Jesus.

Insecurity and Death

IN RECENT YEARS we have become increasingly familiar with the thought of death. We surprise ourselves by the calmness with which we hear of the death of one of our contemporaries. We cannot hate it as we used to, for we have discovered some good in it, and have almost come to terms with it. Fundamentally we feel that we really belong to death already, and that every new day is a miracle. It would probably not be true to say that we welcome death (although we all know that weariness which we ought to avoid like the plague); we are too inquisitive for that—or, to put it more seriously, we should like to see something more of the meaning of our life's broken fragments. Nor do we try to romanticize death, for life is too great and too precious. Still less do we suppose that danger is the meaning of life—we are not desperate enough for that, and we know too much about the good things that life has to offer, though on the other hand we are only too familiar with life's anxieties and with all the other destructive effects of prolonged personal insecurity. We still love life, but I do not think that death can take us by surprise now. After what we have been through during the war, we hardly dare admit that we should like death to come to us, not accidentally and suddenly through some trivial cause, but in the fullness of life and with everything at stake. It is we ourselves, and not outward circumstances, who make death what it can be, a death freely and voluntarily accepted.

The Idolization of Death

...WHEREVER IT IS RECOGNIZED that the power of death has been broken, wherever the world of death is illumined by the miracle of the resurrection and of the new life, there no eternities are demanded of life but one takes of life what it offers, not all or nothing but good and evil, the important and the unimportant, joy and sorrow; one neither clings convulsively to life nor casts it frivolously away. One is content with the allotted span and one does not invest earthly things with the title of eternity; one allows to death the limited rights which it still possesses. It is from beyond death that one expects the coming of the new man and of the new world, from the power by which death has been vanquished.

The risen Christ bears the new humanity within Himself, the final glorious 'yes' which God addresses to the new man. It is true that mankind is still living the old life, but it is already beyond the old. It still lives in a world of death, but it is already beyond death. It still lives in a world of sin, but it is already beyond sin. The night is not yet over, but already the dawn is breaking.

The man whom God has taken to Himself, sentenced and awakened to a new life, this is Jesus Christ. In Him it is all mankind. It is ourselves. Only the form of Jesus Christ confronts the world and defeats it. And it is from this form alone that there comes the formation of a new world, a world which is reconciled with God.

From *The Last Letter*

THESE WILL BE QUIET DAYS in our homes. But I have had the experience over and over again that the quieter it is around me, the clearer do I feel the connection to you. It is as though in solitude the soul develops senses which we hardly know in everyday life. Therefore I have not felt lonely or abandoned for one moment. You, the parents, all of you, the friends and students of mine at the front, all are constantly present to me. Your prayers and good thoughts, words from the Bible, discussions long past,

Editor's note: Written to his fiancée, Maria von Wedemeyer-Weller.

pieces of music, and books,—[all these] gain life and reality as never before. It is a great invisible sphere in which one lives and in whose reality there is no doubt. If it says in the old children's song about the angels: 'Two, to cover me, two, to wake me,' so is this guardianship (*Bewahrung*), by good invisible powers in the morning and at night, something which grown ups need today no less than children. Therefore you must not think that I am unhappy. What is happiness and unhappiness? It depends so little on the circumstances; it depends really only on that which happens inside a person. I am grateful every day that I have you, and that makes me happy (19 December 1944).

Like the Angels

I FEEL that I 'long to look', like the angels in I Peter to see how God is going to solve the apparently insoluble. I think God is about to accomplish something that, even if we take part in it either outwardly or inwardly, we can only receive with the greatest wonder and awe. Somehow it will be clear—for those who have eyes to see—that Ps. 58:11b and Ps. 9:19f[1] are true; and we shall have to repeat Jer. 45:5[2] to ourselves every day.

[1] 'Surely there is a God who judges on the earth.' 'Arise, O Lord! Let not man prevail; let the nations be judged before thee.'

[2] 'And do you seek great things for yourself? Seek them not; for, behold, I am bringing evil upon all flesh, says the Lord; but I will give you your life as a prize of war in all places which you may go.'

His Mercy and Forgiveness

...I AM SO SURE of God's guiding hand that I hope I shall always be kept in that certainty. You must never doubt that I'm travelling with gratitude and cheerfulness along the road where I'm being led. My past life is brim-full of God's goodness, and my sins are covered by the forgiving love of Christ crucified. I'm most thankful for the people I have met, and I only hope that they never have to grieve about me, but that they, too, will always be certain of, and thankful for, God's mercy and forgiveness....

The Hour of Death

...THE HOUR of a man's death is determined, and it will find him no matter where he may turn. We must be ready for it. But

> He knows ten thousand ways
> To save us from death's power.
> He gives us food and meat,
> A boon in famine's hour.

That's something we mustn't forget....

Victory

DEATH is the supreme festival on the road to freedom.

Sources

Bibliography

Christ the Center. London: William Collins & Co., Ltd.; New York: Harper & Row, Publishers, Inc.

Creation and Fall—Temptation. New York: Macmillan Publishing Co., Inc., 1965.

Ethics. New York: Macmillan Publishing Co., Inc., 1965.

Letters and Papers from Prison. New York: Macmillan Publishing Co., Inc., 1972.

Life Together. New York: Harper & Row, Publishers, Inc.

The Cost of Discipleship. New York: Macmillan Publishing Co., Inc., 1963

No Rusty Swords. London: William Collins Sons & Co., Ltd.; New York: Harper & Row, Publishers, Inc.